ROAN MOUNTAIN:
A PASSAGE OF TIME

ROAN MOUNTAIN:
A PASSAGE OF TIME

Jennifer Bauer Wilson

JOHN F. BLAIR, PUBLISHER
Winston-Salem, North Carolina

LIBRARY OF CONGRESS CATALOGING-IN-PUBLICATION DATA

Wilson, Jennifer Bauer,
Roan Mountain : a passage of time / by Jennifer Wilson.
p.   cm.
Includes bibliographical references and index.
ISBN 0-89587-082-7
1. Roan Mountain (N.C. and Tenn.)—History. 2. Roan Mountain
(N.C. and Tenn.)—Description and travel. 3. Natural history—
Roan Mountain (N.C. and Tenn.)   I. Title.
F262.R39W55 1991
976.8'984—dc20

91–9787

For my two lovely daughters,
Carrie and Julia,
who inspired me to complete this book

CONTENTS

PREFACE

*D*uring an especially lush spring in the mid-1970s, I found myself headed for a totally new and refreshing environment. I was nineteen years old, and the upcoming summer was mine to spend at my heart's desire. My destination was Great Smoky Mountains National Park.

Still quite unsure as to what the years ahead might hold, I was hoping that this mountain adventure would provide me with the perfect escape to help me decide just what it was I wanted to do with my life. The southern Appalachians certainly offered a strikingly different atmosphere from that of my home, Baltimore, Maryland.

Loaded down with backpack, sleeping bag, camping equipment, and a small library of university catalogs, I made my way to an obscure campground in the Smokies. Reading and rereading my catalogs, I kept coming back to the sections on elementary education, and I began to get a feeling that I had chosen a career path. Still, I wasn't quite sure.

One warm, breezy day as I sat reading course descriptions, never expecting to see a soul in such isolated surroundings, I was quite surprised when a fellow in a park-service uniform appeared out of nowhere. His name was Troy Brown, and he was the ranger assigned to the particular area where I was staying. After some brief introductions, he offered to show me some special places—spots deep in the mountains where few had ever visited. It seemed a great opportunity to learn about an area that was entirely new to me, so we set off on a day-long exploration.

Every step of our trip presented something different from anything I had ever experienced growing up in a city. We traveled over slick, mossy logs, through rushing creeks, and deep into the woods, discovering old, abandoned dwellings that seemed to call forth images of the families that had long since deserted them. There is no doubt that the places and images from that day made a profound impression on me. But more than that, I was touched by Troy's love for the environment and his commitment to doing whatever he could to protect mountain resources. I even began to share his sense of insult at those moments when we happened upon the assorted trash left by careless campers. As our hike was drawing to a close and we crossed the last bridge to the campground, we stumbled upon a pile of dirty diapers stacked against a tall, graceful hemlock. Apparently, the strain had been too great to carry them to a trash can located just ten feet away! It was as if the perpetrators had littered Troy's personal home; mine, too. From that day onward, I knew what sort of career I wanted to pursue.

That brief summer interlude in the outdoors was just the beginning, creating in me a desire to learn everything I possibly could about plants, animals, and all other subjects having to do with the natural world. That fall, I enrolled at East Tennessee State University as a biology major. After a couple of quarters, it came time to choose an area of concentration within the Biology Department. The decision was an easy one for me, as I was more interested in botany than in any other field. Before long, I was a student worker for the botany professors, and I was taking as many field courses in botany as I could handle.

I had yet to find my way to Roan Mountain. It took a very

special teacher and friend to introduce me to this place so far
removed from my native Baltimore. John Warden, a professor in
the Biology Department, had years before discovered the Roan
and its magnificent and unusual flora and fauna. Anyone who met
him knew immediately that Roan Mountain must be a wonderful
place, for John easily communicated his love and enthusiasm to
students and friends alike. He took me to the Roan many times,
generously sharing his vast knowledge of the mountain's plants
and history. Each trip seemed to leave me wanting more, so upon
the completion of my undergraduate coursework, I immediately
enrolled in the master's program.

My master's thesis was initially intended to follow up work
done by Dr. D. M. Brown on the Roan in the 1930s. Dr. Brown had
provided some of the first scientifically documented material on
the botany of the mountain. Now, fifty years later, I was hoping to
revisit the areas he had photographed, capturing on film the
changes that had taken place over the course of half a century. Yet
one thing led to another. I came to understand that the plants on the
Roan were just one small component of the ecosystem, and that
even documenting the entire ecosystem would fall far short of
capturing the essence of the place. As I dug deeper and deeper into
the literature, I found the human history of the Roan to be
especially interesting. The mountain's earliest inhabited years
were quickly being forgotten as memories faded and important
documentation was stored in attics or relegated to library collections.

Something made me want to preserve the stories, the facts, and
the lost histories of the Roan, for the mountain's past was anything
but ordinary. I spent every spare moment I could find immersed in
library microfilm, microfiche, and rare-book collections. Every
old paper and text I discovered seemed to refer me to other early
writers, turning my research into a scavenger hunt through time.
It was amazing how much history on the Roan had been written
and filed away through the years, even if it was in bits and pieces.

Still, there were gaps in the story of Roan Mountain that could only be filled in by local people themselves. I began searching for those people born before the turn of the century, people with personal knowledge of earlier days, and then I broadened my hunt to include those whose elders had at least left memories and tales with them. Again, I found that each of my contacts sent me to others. Some I reached by mail and some in person. All were more than eager to share their experiences and recollections. An unexpected blessing was the great number of old photographs documenting earlier times on Roan Mountain that many of my contacts were willing to pass along.

In the midst of all this work, and while I was still trying to complete my degree, an odd twist of fate occurred. John Warden informed me that an interview committee from the Tennessee State Parks system was coming to East Tennessee State. They were hiring seasonal naturalists for three-month positions. I decided to give it a try and was lucky enough to be hired to work that summer in a park in Kingsport. The following summer, I was transferred to the Roan, and before long I was working full-time as a ranger naturalist at Roan Mountain State Park. Opportunities for meeting area people and for conducting my own research into the history of the Roan then became abundant. A chronicle of the mountain and the people who have called it their home began to fall into place.

This book attempts to impose a sense of order upon a random collection of misplaced photographs, notes, partial histories, scientific data, and local tales. It is hoped that the end result will be judged worthy of its subject, one of the most popular places in the Southeast today.

Warm thanks are due the many people who shared their knowledge of Roan Mountain with me. There were also a number of folks who mailed me pictures or left them on my desk without ever identifying themselves, and their kindness is also appreciated. A very special thank-you goes out to John Warden and Thomas O.

Maher, whose encouragement inspired my efforts at documenting Roan Mountain's history. And finally, I would like to thank the fine folks at John F. Blair, Publisher, for working with me and guiding me through this book. I had wanted for years to see the story of the Roan preserved in book form, and without their support it would not have been possible.

ROAN MOUNTAIN:
A PASSAGE OF TIME

View of Round Bald (in foreground) across Engine Gap toward Jane Bald and Grassy Ridge Bald, 1900

GEOGRAPHY

$\mathcal{T}$he southern section of the Appalachians is divided into two major mountain ranges, the Unaka Mountains to the west and the Blue Ridge Mountains to the east. The two ranges run roughly parallel to each other, extending northeast and southwest. A number of cross ranges are oriented southward from the Unakas to the Blue Ridge. Located at a latitude of 82 degrees west and a longitude of 36 degrees north, Roan Mountain is one of the highest of those cross ranges.

There are a variety of explanations that attempt to account for Roan Mountain's name, none of which has gained a wide acceptance. Some people claim that the mountain appears a distinct roan color when its trademark Catawba rhododendron is in full bloom in late June and early July, and thus the name. Others say that Daniel Boone was a frequent visitor to the mountain on his excursions in the high country, and that the mountain received its name as a tribute to Boone's roan-colored horse. Another theory involves the local population of mountain ash trees, whose vibrant red berries make the forests come alive during the autumn; the mountain ash was known as the rowan tree in days past, the theory goes, and that name eventually came to be applied to the entire mountain, with the *w* dropped from popular usage over the course of time. One stubborn legend has it that André Michaux, a famous French botanist and one of the earliest men to document the southern Appalachians, was inspired to name the mountain after his native Rhone Valley while gazing upon its scenery one particularly lovely day. The spelling was later altered from *Rhone* because early settlers thought Michaux must have been referring to the mountain's roan color and misspelling the name himself. It should be noted, however, that Michaux was not a native of the Rhone Valley.

It is every bit as difficult to categorize the Roan as it is to account for the origin of its name. I had visited a number of peaks in the southern Appalachians before I made my first trip to Roan Mountain, and I noticed that most of the other summits rose to a high peak, often topped with a fire tower or an overlook. Once

Bygone traffic on the Doe River, 1880s

*A pair of General John T. Wilder's horses, Comet and Jupiter,
about to cross Hampton Creek, 1880s*

you'd climbed the tower or partaken of the view, you'd seen pretty
much everything there was to be seen.

   Such is not the case with Roan Mountain, and I suppose that is
part of the reason why it continues to impress me to this day. The
Roan does not simply end at a high peak. Rather, its long, high
ridge, or "summit," spreads in waves for more than five miles.
Roan Mountain proper encompasses approximately twelve square
miles, but if the entire surface area created by the mountain mass
is taken into consideration, then that total area is more like fifty
square miles. The altitude at the base of the Roan is approximately
2,500 feet. The ridge line, or "summit," ranges from a high of
6,285 feet at Roan High Knob to a low of 5,500 feet at Carver's
Gap. Rounded spurs and broad, V-shaped valleys are situated on
either side of the ridge line. To the west, the area is drained by the
Doe River, while to the east, it is drained by the Toe River, both

Road along the Doe, 1880s

of which empty into the Tennessee River.

The easy confusion between the Doe and the Toe and the fact that Roan Mountain is not a single peak but a long, high ridge make things difficult enough on the first-time visitor, but matters are further complicated by the fact that the Tennessee–North Carolina boundary runs along the ridge line. Many newcomers have been left to ponder whether particular overlooks give a view into the Volunteer State or Tar Heel country. They are sometimes uncertain where points of interest near the ridge line are located in relation to the border, or even whether they themselves are standing or driving in Tennessee or North Carolina at a given time.

To put things in perspective, it might be said that most of the commerce and human activity in the immediate area is concentrated on the Tennessee side, while many of the notable natural features of the Roan itself are to be found on the North Carolina side.

The closest sizable town in either state is Johnson City, Tennessee. Most visitors approaching Roan Mountain from the Tennessee side take Highway 19E from Elizabethton, a road that climbs through the small communities of Valley Forge, Hampton, and Crabtree to the village of Roan Mountain, Tennessee, situated at the base of the mountain. The village of Roan Mountain is a pleasant mixture of the old and the new. Historic buildings dating back to the nineteenth century line the old Main Street. For example, the S. B. Woods Pharmacy, dating to 1898, still operates on Highway 19E. Directly across from it are two antique shops located in buildings that date to the same period. Along the old Main Street, which intersects Highway 19E across from the Carter County Bank, the old theater and early stores are mixed in with renovated nineteenth-century homes. The newer eateries and grocery stores are clear signs of changing times.

Travelers who continue on Highway 19E reach the North Carolina border after only five miles, but those who wish to proceed the twenty-two miles to the top of the mountain should

View across the Doe into the village of Roan Mountain, 1880s

An 1888 view of the village, with the roof of the Roan Mountain Inn in the foreground

follow the prominent signs for Roan Mountain State Park and the Rhododendron Gardens visible at the main intersection in the village of Roan Mountain.

After turning onto Tennessee Highway 143, it is approximately four miles to the entrance of Roan Mountain State Park, a resort park created in the 1950s and developed in the 1970s. Park visitors can enjoy camping and a variety of recreational activities. Cabins are also available for rent. Leaving the park, the climb begins in earnest. As the road winds its way upward, the views open up to reveal astonishing vistas back into Tennessee, primarily toward Johnson City; on clear nights, it is easy to see car lights around Johnson City on I-181. There is an intersection at the top of Roan Mountain. The road to the right, maintained by the United States Forest Service, stretches for three miles along the crest of the ridge.

Boone, Banner Elk, Blowing Rock, and Grandfather Mountain are some of the main attractions in North Carolina within an hour

View from Carver's Gap into North Carolina

View from the Rhododendron Gardens into North Carolina, 1930s

east of Roan Mountain; that area of the mountains is popular among tourists in the summer and skiers in the winter. Visitors approaching Roan Mountain from the east and northeast generally find their way to Elk Park, North Carolina, then follow Highway 19E across the Tennessee line to the village of Roan Mountain, then proceed up to the crest on Tennessee Highway 143. Those approaching from farther south in the Tar Heel State make the climb through a portion of the Pisgah National Forest on North Carolina Highway 261 from Bakersville, the closest community on the North Carolina side. North Carolina Highway 261 meets Tennessee Highway 143 and the United States Forest Service road at the state border at the crest of Roan Mountain.

That intersection is an important one. It falls near the center of what is known as "the highlands of the Roan," with a roughly equal number of the mountain's principal attractions to the southwest and the northeast. It also marks an intersection with the Appalachian Trail, which rides the Tennessee–North Carolina

The Pumpkin Patch Mountains of North Carolina, taken from below Carver's Gap, 1930s

View from Round Bald into Carver's Gap today

border through that section of the mountains. The Appalachian Trail is the longest continuous marked trail in the world, stretching some two thousand miles from Georgia's Springer Mountain to Maine's Mount Katahdin. En route, it traverses some of the finest country east of the Mississippi, including eight national forests, two national parks, a number of state parks, and a good deal of private land as well. The place where the state highways and the Forest Service road converge is known as Carver's Gap, named for John Carver. Carver was a familiar figure in the gap in days gone by, as it was his favorite site for grazing his flocks of sheep.

Visitors who turn onto the Forest Service road at Carver's Gap pass through a lush forest of spruce and fir that covers Roan High Knob, the highest point on the mountain. Along the road, clearings

"The hotel property and mountain are surrounded by a fence ten miles long entered by three gates," advertisements for the Cloudland Hotel used to boast. Though the evidence has long since disappeared, this site in Carver's Gap was the location of one of the gates onto the Cloudland property.

View of Carver's Gap from Round Bald in the direction of Roan High Knob

and small grassy areas provide places for picnics and great views into the North Carolina mountains. Occasional trails lead from the gravel pull-offs back into the forest. Farther along, the road forks. The right fork leads to a parking lot that overlooks Tennessee and to the former site of the Cloudland Hotel, the spectacular edifice that brought Roan Mountain its greatest fame back around the turn of the century. The left fork leads to the Rhododendron Gardens, perhaps the most popular natural feature of the Roan today. The gardens offer more than two hundred acres of Catawba rhododendron, the largest such expanse in the United States. Visitors flock to see the beautiful red colors in late June or early July.

Bygone traffic through Carver's Gap

Part of the old road leading from Carver's Gap toward Cloudland

Carver's Gap today

Past the Rhododendron Gardens, there is a loop in the road, and at the far end of the loop is the start of a foot trail that leads to Roan High Bluff. Roan High Bluff marks the beginning of a series of high rock cliffs and ridges that highlights the southwest end of the Roan. Charles Lanman visited the mountain in the middle part of the nineteenth century and recorded his impression of Roan High Bluff in *Letters from the Alleghany Mountains*: "The ascent to the top of this peak is gradual from all directions except one, but on the north it is quite perpendicular, and to one standing near the brow of the mighty cliff the scene is exceedingly imposing and fearful." Both the Rhododendron Gardens and Roan High Bluff fall on the North Carolina side of the border.

Roan Mountain is famous partly because of its large balds— areas that remain free of trees for no apparent reason. The Roan's

This formation on Roan High Bluff was formerly known as the Roan Sphinx, or Profile Rock. It was said to resemble President William McKinley. The formation can no longer be seen today.

Roan High Bluff

View of Round Bald across Carver's Gap around 1930

principal balds lie northeast of the place where the state highways and the Forest Service road converge, and they are accessible from Carver's Gap only by trail. In fact, it is a hike of about fourteen miles from Carver's Gap before another road is reached.

The first bald past Carver's Gap is Round Bald, which sits above Engine Gap, named for the steam engine based there in the early part of this century that transported cherry lumber from Tennessee to the Champion company's paper mill in Canton, North Carolina. Past Engine Gap is Jane Bald, which boasts abundant rock outcroppings and rhododendron. The story goes that in days gone by, a woman named Jane was traveling from Tennessee across Roan Mountain to visit relatives in North Carolina. Unbeknownst to her at the start of her journey, she had

View of Roan High Knob from the Rhododendron Gardens

contracted milk sickness, a disease brought on by drinking milk from cattle that have been poisoned by eating certain kinds of snakeroot. Little-known today, milk sickness was often fatal in times past, and such was the case with the woman named Jane. She died on the bald that now bears her name.

Beyond Jane Bald is Grassy Ridge Bald—formerly known as Chair Rock Bald—and then Yellow Mountain and Hump Mountain, which are not considered part of Roan Mountain proper, though they are part of the general area called "the highlands of the Roan." The Overmountain Men—the Revolutionary War soldiers who came across the mountains to defeat the British at Kings Mountain, South Carolina, in 1780—traversed Yellow Mountain and Hump Mountain on their historic march. Past Hump Mountain, hikers finally begin their descent to Highway 19E just above the village of Roan Mountain.

Roan Mountain is a uniquely interesting place, as the great majority of its visitors will attest. Shared by Tennessee and North Carolina, it attracts guests from well beyond the boundaries of those two states. People come to hike the balds, to see the rhodo-dendron in bloom, to enjoy the fall colors, and to camp and picnic at the state park. Though it is easily accessible, the Roan is really a world unto itself. For example, the mountain is less than fifty miles from Johnson City, yet the growing season in its highlands is more than a month shorter than Johnson City's; and during a good winter season, the Roan may boast a two-foot base of natural snow. Whatever the reasons for their initial visits, people who make the trek to Roan Mountain generally come back again and again.

A rare photo from the 1880s documenting that Roan High Bluff was once nearly bald. The sphagnum moss visible on the rocks is evidence of the effects of glaciers.

*T*he Appalachian Mountains were formed approximately 400 million years ago, when the moving continental plates of North America and Africa collided along what is now the east coast of the United States. The entire process of buckling, fracturing, and uplifting is believed to have taken about 50 million years.

The rocks that make up Roan Mountain actually predate the formation of the Appalachians. The oldest variety is called Cranberry gneiss. Dated at more than a billion years, it is among the oldest rocks to be found in the United States. As a point of reference, it is believed by many scientists that the most advanced forms of life on earth at that time were sponges, coral, and jellyfish. Cranberry gneiss consists of pink feldspar layered with thin bands of dark mica. Another of the dominant rocks on the mountain is Roan gneiss, dated at about 800 million years. Like Cranberry gneiss, it is classified as metamorphic rock. Roan gneiss is a green-black hornblende rock with thin bands of dark gray mica. The variety of igneous rock known as Beech granite, a reddish-colored rock dated at 700 million years, is also much in evidence.

Geologists believe that the peaks in the vicinity of Roan

Mountain may have been as high as twenty to thirty thousand feet before the slow processes of glaciation and erosion brought them to their present height over the course of many millions of years.

It is glaciation that is given a large share of the credit for the Roan's unique flora. Oak-chestnut forests dominate the mountain below thirty-five hundred feet, with beech-maple forests gaining preeminence between thirty-five hundred and five thousand feet in altitude. The glaciers exerted their principal impact in the spruce-fir forests that are found above five thousand feet, giving rise to an area of unusual vegetation known as "the Canadian zone."

During the geological time period called the Wisconsin Glaciation, glaciers reached their farthest point south before warming weather made them begin to retreat northward. With the movement of ice through and beyond Tennessee and the Carolinas, arctic and Canadian plant and animal species migrated southward, as the southern climate began to mimic that of lands far to the north. Before the retreat, the Fraser fir, a soft evergreen most common today in the far northeastern United States and in Canada, was thriving as far south as Florida. With the coming of warmer weather, the retreating glaciers left behind remnants of their travels—a number of rare and endangered plants that are considered to be Canadian species. Isolated atop the Roan and other mountains of similar height, they are unable to spread because of their need for high elevation, a cool climate, and a short growing season.

John Strother, a member of the team that surveyed the Tennessee–North Carolina state line in 1799, commented on the visual effect of the Canadian zone: "As one ascends . . . the size of all the trees perceptibly diminish, especially near the 6,000 foot line, to be succeeded, generally, on the less precipitous slopes, by miniature beech trees, perfect in shape, but resembling the so called dwarf trees of the Japanese. They really seem to be toy trees."

First-time visitors to the Roan are likely to be pleasantly surprised at the Canadian zone's cool climate during the summer months. It is not unusual for the temperature to drop thirty degrees as a midsummer thunderstorm approaches. The surprise may not be so pleasant if they happen to visit during the harsh, unforgiving winters, when temperatures may reach twenty-five degrees below zero. The growing season on the high reaches of the mountain is limited to a little more than three months of the year. Moisture level and winds are higher and snows are deeper than at lower elevations.

The plant communities of the Canadian zone attracted some of the most important botanists in the world to Roan Mountain in the eighteenth and nineteenth centuries, and they continue to attract both professional and amateur plant lovers today. Above five thousand feet, the beech-maple forests give way to spruce-fir forests. Inexperienced hikers on the Roan often find it astonishing that the composition of the forest should change so completely over the course of a half-mile's walking distance, or even less on steep slopes. From certain lookout points at high altitudes, visitors can see the transitional areas where deciduous trees become dwarfed and finally disappear, only to be replaced by the spruce and fir. Some scientists have attempted to ascribe the hardiness of the spruce and fir to the presence of a high content of fatty substances manufactured by their leaves. Fatty materials, the theory goes, depress the freezing point, and they also help cells retain their water when it would otherwise be drawn out by the presence of ice.

Red spruce trees are growing more numerous than firs in the Canadian-zone forests. The spruce is distinguished by its four-sided, sharp-pointed needles. The Fraser fir is distinguished by its flat, soft, two-sided needles, which have a whitish underside. Firs were once more numerous than spruce trees on the Roan, but they have died off considerably in recent years due to infestation by an insect called the woolly balsam aphid. Still, the forest floor is a tes-

Hiker in virgin Fraser fir forest on the Roan

tament to the firs' ability to survive; their seedlings are as thick as a carpet as they try to regain their rightful place in the spruce-fir zone.

Purple wood sorrel is a small, cloverlike herb whose flowers illuminate the deep shade during midsummer. It is among the many notable species present in the high forests. Clinton's lily, with its wide leaves and soft, yellow blooms, grows in thick patches in places where filtered sunlight reaches the ground. On warm, damp summer days, hikers in the forests may happen upon an array of mushrooms that boasts every color in the rainbow.

The other notable feature of the Canadian zone is the Rhododendron Gardens, located past Roan High Knob toward the southwest part of the Roan. News of the gardens' beauty has spread far and wide, so that now thousands upon thousands of people flock to the mountain at the peak bloom period during the summer. In a good year, a single bush might boast over a hundred clusters of flowers, while hundreds of bushes spread out over the mountainside. Catawba rhododendron bushes are so plump and round that it appears they must have been pruned by the hand of man to achieve their perfect shape, yet the only sculpture at work on Roan Mountain is that of mother nature. At first, visitors are captivated by the broad panorama of beautiful crimson, but if they care to look closely enough, they may find the rhododendron just as fascinating upon close examination of an individual flower. Each petal is sprinkled with an intricate pattern of tiny spots along its lip that acts as a kind of runway for bees circling and looking for a flower to pollinate. Rhododendron bushes also spread via their root systems.

It takes a keen eye to pick out some of the tinier species in the Rhododendron Gardens, but the rewards are great. As small as the tip of a baby's finger, the flower of the rare dwarf plant called enchanter's nightshade must be seen nose to nose to be appreciated. The plants' leaves appear to be quilted; they cover the ground beneath the rhododendron. Gray's lily is a rare, beautiful

Wood sorrel and Fraser fir seedlings

Clinton's lily

Catawba rhododendron at its finest

Bee inspecting rhododendron

red flower with a black-spotted throat. Mountain ash, elderberry, gooseberry, mountain avens, Michaux's saxifrage, and many other plants also make their home in the Rhododendron Gardens. Special areas of transition occur in places where the older rhododendron shrubs are being overtaken by evergreens. With the rhododendron bent into bizarre, twisted shapes, the aura is much like the enchanted forest of children's storybooks.

No discussion of the vegetation on Roan Mountain can be complete without an attempt to unravel the mystery of the balds, areas whose lack of forest growth defies explanation. Such areas speckle the Roan and the rest of the southern Appalachians rather liberally, but they are exceedingly uncommon elsewhere.

There are two basic types of balds, with numerous variations. Areas populated only by grasses, weeds, and wildflowers are known as grass balds. Areas that support the growth of shrubs are called shrub balds or heath balds. The Rhododendron Gardens

This 1897 view shows the prominence of Roan Mountain's balds in days past. The old road can be seen meandering across the high ridge, with Roan High Knob in the upper center. The entire area is forested today.

constitute the major shrub bald on Roan Mountain. The grass balds are more extensive, and they are all situated northwest of Carver's Gap—Round Bald, Jane Bald, Grassy Ridge Bald, and Hump Mountain, or "the Hump," as it is popularly known. The Roan's balds are located on long, broad ridges above fifty-five hundred feet in altitude. They cover an area of more than a thousand acres, mostly with a southern exposure.

Early visitors to Roan Mountain commented on its prominent balds. In fact, the unusual vegetation on the balds played a large part in making the Roan a haven for the botanist-explorers of the eighteenth and nineteenth centuries. Botanist Elisha Mitchell, for example, wrote of being able to ride his horse for several miles along the crest without encountering a tree to obstruct his view.

Balds are not entirely static; plant succession does occur on them. Old photographs reveal that Roan High Knob was once an open meadow with rhododendron thickets on the side. Photos taken over the course of the past hundred years show that the tree line was substantially lower on the mountain in years gone by, especially on the North Carolina side. This suggests that the balds are slowly being encroached upon by larger plant species, and that prudent management of the fragile, beautiful ecosystem of the balds will become increasingly necessary as the years pass.

The Cherokee Indians have a legend that accounts for the origin of the balds. They say that there was once a giant yellow jacket known as Ulagu that terrorized a particular Cherokee village by swooping down, carrying off young children, and flying away faster than the village's warriors could follow. After much anguish, the Indians hit upon the idea of posting sentinels along the tops of mountains as a means of tracking Ulagu's flight to its home. That accomplished, the Cherokees prayed to the Great Spirit for aid, and the Great Spirit obliged by sending a bolt of lightning to split open the mountain where Ulagu lived. The warriors then proceeded to hunt down the beast and kill it. So pleased was the Great Spirit by the Cherokees' resourcefulness, by

View across a small farm to Roan High Knob

A 1938 shot of conifers invading the Catawba rhododendron

their piety in beseeching him for help, and by their bravery in finally killing Ulagu that he rewarded them by keeping the tops of the mountains bare of trees, so they could serve as sentry posts should the need ever arise again.

Early white settlers in the mountains had their own legends about the origin of the balds, many of them centering around the devil. It was said that balds came about whenever the devil went walking in the mountains, with each of his footsteps causing the growth to be permanently stunted.

Scientific theories have ranged from the mundane to the preposterous. Scientists have long lined up to offer their pet explanations, or to take turns poking holes in each other's theories. In *The Natural Gardens of North Carolina*, Bertram Whittier Wells summed up the scientific community's frustration in trying to account for the origin of the balds: "Why this hesitancy to go back to forest when forests are all around them? In all the rest of the state when a treeless area is left undisturbed it is but a matter of from five to twenty years until the pines begin to take it, and on most sites, if no fire comes, the oak-hickory or oak-chestnut forest will follow the pines. It may thus be seen that the balds are all out of joint with the rest of our vegetation; they ought to disappear but they don't." Despite the best efforts of a good many bright minds, no completely satisfactory theory has ever been offered.

One school of scientific thought favored natural causes. Helen R. Edson was among the very first to try to explain the balds. Mrs. Edson, a New Yorker, was surely one of the hardiest visitors ever on the Roan. One year in the 1880s, she stayed through the winter in a small cabin atop the mountain so she could document the effects of cold and moisture at high altitude. At the end of her study, she published an article entitled "Frost Forms on Roan Mountain," complete with photographs showing frost buildup on the vegetation. In a 1903 paper entitled "An Ecological Study of the Mountainous North Carolina," J. C. Harshberger summarized her findings: "Mrs. Edson describes the action of a winter storm

Helen R. Edson (center) and friends at her cabin near the Cloudland Hotel

upon the vegetation. The factor in the production of the frost forms which weigh down the limbs of trees and snap them off is the frozen vapor of the wind and rain. The lower the temperature, the denser the cloud becomes; the velocity of the wind and the exposure determine the growth on the frost forms. Hence the absence of trees is due to the effect of the ice and snow of winter."

Harshberger went on to add that "wherever the topography is such as to permit the full force of the ice storm, there tree vegetation is scanty or altogether wanting, and its place is taken by grassy stretches, or by thickets of alder and rhododendron, plants which are adapted to withstand ice storms." Subsequent research has failed to find a direct causal connection between harsh weather and the balds, however.

Other natural-cause theories have ascribed the balds to soil acidity or fires, but they have failed to address the issue of how either could bring about the sharp demarcation that characterizes the balds. The forest does not thin at the edge of a bald; rather, the line between a bald and the surrounding forest is as distinct as if it were the product of human clearing. Extensive soil-acidity tests have failed to prove that balds are infertile. In 1957, W. D. Billings and A. F. Mark of Duke University proposed a theory that natural balds occur only in forest margins. Every tree species has an upper and lower altitude limit, and it was Billings and Mark's contention that balds arise at the edge of the tolerance range of the dominant tree in a particular forest. While their theory may have been a good starting point, it did not address why balds fail to develop in marginal zones where the conditions of soil, climate, altitude, and forest composition are identical to those at the site of existing balds.

William H. Gates of Louisiana State University proposed an elaborate theory. Gates's research was concentrated on and around Wine Spring Bald and Wayah Bald, eighteen miles west of Franklin, North Carolina—or about a hundred miles from Roan Mountain—but so confident was he that he sought to extrapolate

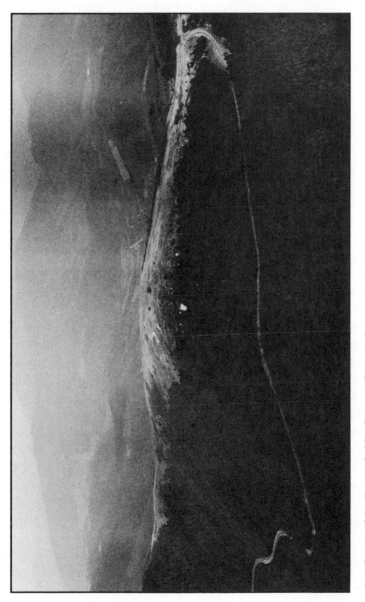

Aerial view of the Roan's balds. Carver's Gap can be seen to the right.

his findings to account for balds throughout the southern Appalachians.

During the course of his camping vacations on Wine Spring Bald over the course of eight consecutive summers, Gates observed the infestation of a local population of red oaks by an insect identified as the twig-gall wasp. During the larval stage of their development, the wasps pushed their way through the bark and twigs of the oaks, so many of them that the trees were effectively girdled and killed. Gates observed that the infestation had a very sharply defined border visible at a distance of two or three miles, and that all trees within the effected area were victims. And it just so happened that the twig-gall wasp's altitude range corresponded fairly closely to the high and low altitudes between which balds throughout the southern Appalachians are generally found—from three thousand to six thousand feet.

Gates could not seem to emphasize the destructive power of the wasps strongly enough. "It is impossible to describe the attack of these wasps adequately," he wrote. "Practically *every* twig of *every* oak was infested. . . . When one considers the thousands of oaks involved, the total number of insects becomes incalculable." Later, he noted, "It is utterly impossible to give any conception of the almost infinite number of gall larvae that were to be found on Wayah Bald and Wine Spring Bald." Indeed, so impressed was Gates that he refused to let contrary observations stand in the way of what he knew in his heart was good theory. When he failed to find evidence of twig-gall wasps on any other balds, he speculated that it was precisely the insect's tendency to hit-and-run that left other balds free of damning proof; in a case of circular reasoning, what should have been a fly in his theory's ointment became instead further proof of its correctness. A more important point Gates missed was that wasp infestation could not cause the *permanent* absence of trees on balds.

Another school of thought ascribed the balds to human activity. In 1936, B. W. Wells theorized that they were the sites of old

Indian campgrounds used during the summertime. As evidence, he cited the facts that Indians preferred ridge trails for travel and hunting and that good sources of drinking water are commonly found at the lower margins of balds. However, Wells's argument failed to address why the balds should remain long after their use as Indian campsites was ended. He also neglected to consider the variety of Indian legends that seek to explain the origin of the balds; the balds were a mystery to the Indians, too, and they obviously predated the Indians' presence in the mountains.

A related theory suggested that the balds were cleared by humans—whether Indians or white settlers—as game lures. While such lures may have had some utility in the hunting of some animals, like wild turkeys, the fact remains that most balds are situated above the altitude range of the white-tailed deer, one of the principal game animals in the southern Appalachians. Many deer are to be found in valleys and on the lower slopes of the mountains, but seldom will one venture as high as the balds.

Sheep grazing among the rhododendron bushes, 1930s

Burning and grazing certainly contributed to the persistence of the balds, even if they could not have caused them in the first place. A great deal of burning occurred on the Roan throughout the nineteenth century and up to about 1930. "I can still see the black spring smokes a-risin' from the top of the mountain," recalled one old-timer from the North Carolina side, who went on to explain that burning was intended to thicken up the grass for grazing. Old photographs document the grazing of sheep on the Roan. The grazing areas were widely scattered, from the Rhododendron Gardens clear across the balds to Grassy Ridge. Grazing did have a positive side. It kept the balds and their magnificent views open and clear, since livestock prevented beech trees, blackberries, and other small trees and shrubs from gaining a foothold in their pasture area. Yet at the same time, erosion and trampling became a problem. Holes and ditches formed along the ridges. Small, delicate tundra species were damaged or destroyed by the constant trampling. J. H. Redfield noted in 1879 that "much of the summit prairie flora has doubtless been destroyed by the large herds of cattle, horses, and sheep which are every summer sent to the mountain top for pasture." The welfare of the Roan's supply of Gray's lily was of particular concern. That rare plant was especially vulnerable because it grows in open bald meadows. J. W. Chickering noted in 1880 that "the persistent and careful search of all the botanists, with efficient help from many others, brought to light only ten specimens [of Gray's lily]; all growing in clumps of Alder or Rhododendron, and thus protected against cattle, sheep, and goats, those enemies of all botanists, who bid that in distant time to exterminate it from the Roan."

The effects of grazing were still much in evidence on Roan Mountain fifty years after Chickering's day. Paul Fink noted in *Backpacking Was the Only Way* that "the whole top of the mountain was a veritable maze of sheep and cattle paths." Again, it should be noted that burning and grazing could not have *caused* the balds, since the balds were in existence before human habitation.

J. W. Chickering characterized sheep, along with cattle and goats, as "those enemies of all botanists"

One of the most comprehensive and believable theories on the balds takes both natural and human influences into consideration. During the time when glaciers covered the southern Appalachians, many tundra and Canadian species found their way to the high mountains in the area, species typically found only many hundreds of miles to the north. Only the tallest of the Appalachian peaks could continue supporting the new species after the glaciers retreated, and they thus became isolated in pockets. With the coming of humans, the pockets containing northern vegetation became the logical places to instigate the practices of burning and grazing, since those areas were more sparsely populated by plant life than the surrounding country. Burning and grazing then played a role in keeping the balds open until the present. Still, it remains to be explained why some balds are located at lower elevations and in warmer local climates than are some areas that are heavily forested. Taken as a whole, the balds are random dots on the high peaks of the southern Appalachians, with no particular rhyme or reason to their placement. Perhaps the only definite thing that can be said about the balds is that their cause will remain a mystery for many years to come.

Roan Mountain's fauna is probably less renowned than its flora, but there are still many interesting animal species in residence, ranging from snow fleas to bobcats. Several small mammals considered endangered have found the Roan the perfect place to survive. Among them are the least weasel, the woodland jumping mouse, the Smokey shrew, and the Southern bog lemming. The elusive Eastern spotted skunk may also be sighted infrequently, as may the Northern flying squirrel, a resident of the spruce-fir forests. The tiniest of the owls, the saw-whet, can reproduce only in those high forests.

Face-to-face encounters with wildlife can sometimes be a little too thrilling, which may help explain why some of us naturalists lean toward botany. I remember one late-summer day on the Roan several years ago when the weather had turned as cool and crisp as fall. It seemed a perfect day for a little adventuring, so I headed out with a friend and her dog to an area of high cliffs rich in beautiful plants—one of my favorite places for exploring and relaxing. Getting there was a real challenge. The first part of the hike was an easy walk along a gravel road, but once the road ended it was necessary to follow the high ridge line, which was completely overgrown and piled high with downed trees; winds at the top of the Roan are so strong and the soil layer so thin that trees sometimes drop as if they were no more substantial than blades of grass. It took us a full forty-five minutes to crawl through a painful seventy-five feet of trees, briers, and the like. The rest of the hike was relatively easy, as the ridge top was lined with huge rocks and rock shelters. What stood out in my mind more than anything else was an odd odor that overcame us at one point in our travels—it was musky, and a little like a wet dog. My friend and I commented on it and plodded onward.

Once we reached our destination, we spent the day basking in the sun, snacking, and watching the ravens circling above us. As daylight began to wane, we realized we'd better start scrambling back if we wanted to get through the overgrown areas before dark.

The walk back was quiet, especially since we were too tired and lazy to feel obliged to move quickly. An evening breeze began to stir, and I suddenly noticed the strange odor again. I asked my companion if she, too, smelled it, but before she could answer we found ourselves face to face with her dog—closely followed by a mother bear and her cub! In a flash, I recalled my wildlife lessons. Lesson number one says that a hiker should never run from a bear, since bears can outrun humans. Yet before I could come up with a reasonable alternative to running, my friend yelled, "Let's get out of here!" and was off at top speed. Wildlife lessons to the contrary, I was instantly hot on her trail.

How we managed to negotiate our way through the trees and briers I will never know, but I do know that we whittled our previous time of forty-five minutes down to ten minutes. And I never felt a single brier, either. When we finally paused to assess the situation, we were joined by my friend's dog, none the worse for wear, and fortunately *without* his fan club.

I'm confident I will remember that musky, wet-dog odor if there ever is a next time. With hunting pressures, and with so many communities and homes occupying the black bear's old range, those magnificent animals sometimes find it difficult to hold their own. It is thrilling to know that they are still living in the mountains. They manage quite well in the more secluded areas of the Roan.

The special environment on Roan Mountain is one that is able to sustain some of the most rare and interesting plant and animal species to be found anywhere. Even those visitors who have come to the mountain time and again still find ample opportunities for discovery whenever they look closely enough to see.

$\mathcal{T}$he first settlers in the Roan Mountain area were Indians. Legends have long held an important place in Indian culture. Things not completely understood were often explained through stories and tales. Roan Mountain was a place of mystery to the Indians, since its open balds made it distinctly different from the surrounding peaks. They found it to be a fitting subject for legend.

The Catawbas have an important legend about the Roan. It is said that in days long past, when territory was hotly disputed among the Indian tribes, the Catawbas challenged the Cherokees and all their other foes to a great battle atop the mountain. The prize for the victors was the right to lay claim to the Roan itself. Days passed without an end in sight, and it began to appear hopeless that a winner would ever emerge. Finally, it was the Catawbas who stepped forward and overtook the other tribes. Not wanting such a great battle to go unremembered, the Great Spirit caused the forest to wither from the spots where fighting had taken place. Then the rhododendron, nourished by the blood of the many

A legend among the Catawba Indians has it that the rhododendron atop the Roan turned from white to red after a great battle. This view is from the 1940s.

A 1946 view of visitors exploring the Catawba rhododendron

hundreds who were slain, turned from white to the beautiful crimson seen today. And in fact, when the Roan's trademark rhododendron was given a botanical name many years later, it was christened *Rhododendron catawbiense*, or Catawba rhododendron, perhaps to honor the victors of that legendary battle.

No proof of such events exists, of course, but there is evidence of Indian settlement at scattered locations around the base of the Roan. Some of the gaps in the mountain were used for traveling between what are now Tennessee and North Carolina, but the high ridge of the Roan was too cold for year-round habitation, so artifacts are more difficult to come by along the peak.

The first men to explore the southern Appalachians in systematic fashion were the botanists of the eighteenth and nineteenth centuries. Some of them traveled under the sponsorship of European governments. Nurseries were set up in North America to care for the plants they discovered until they could be carefully packaged and shipped across the Atlantic, at which time they became sources of national pride in the gardens of France, Russia, and other countries.

Today, it may seem a little difficult to understand the urge that moved men to venture to distant lands and sometimes risk life and limb in their efforts to discover new plant species. John Bartram, a Pennsylvania farmer born in 1699 who became the first man to attempt to catalog plant life in the southern Appalachians, eloquently captured the spirit of discovery of his time:

> One day I was very busy in holding my plough . . .
> and being weary, I ran under the shade of a tree to
> repose myself. I cast my eyes on a *daisy*; I plucked it
> mechanically, and viewed it with more curiosity than
> common country farmers are wont to do, and
> observed therein very many distinct parts, some
> perpendicular—some horizontal. *What a shame*, said
> my mind, or something that inspired my mind, *that
> thee shouldst have employed so many years in tilling*

the earth, and destroying so many flowers and plants,
without being acquainted with their structures and
their uses! This seeming inspiration suddenly
awakened my curiousity [*sic*], for these were not
thoughts to which I had been accustomed. I returned
to my team, but this new desire did not quit my mind;
I mentioned it to my wife, who greatly discouraged
me from prosecuting my new scheme, as she called it;
I was not opulent enough, she said, to dedicate much
of my time to studies and labors which might rob me
of that portion of it which is the only wealth of the
American farmer. However, her prudent caution did
not discourage me; I thought about it continually,—at
supper, in bed, and wherever I went. At last, I could
not resist the impulse.

Bartram's botanical excursions took him through Maryland,
Virginia, the Carolinas, and as far as Florida. After a time, he
could justifiably boast that "by a steady application of several
years, I have acquired a pretty general knowledge of every plant
and tree to be found in our Continent." The difficulty of traveling
by horse and foot through new territories in those days cannot be
underestimated. It must have taken a special kind of resolve to
tackle high mountains like the Roan. Bartram's letters describe
the rigors of surviving in the backwoods of the southern Appalachians in vivid detail. Insects were a problem, as were wild
animals. "The panthers have not seized any of our people, that I
have heard," Bartram wrote in 1738. "But many have been sadly
frightened with them. They have pursued several men, both on
horseback and foot. Many have shot them down, and others have
escaped by running away."

The spirit of exploration must have gotten into the Bartram
blood. John Bartram's son, William, followed in his father's
footsteps. In 1773, William began a four-year botanical excursion
in the Southeast under the sponsorship of a prominent London
physician, Dr. John Fothergill. His journeys found him in the

View from the Rhododendron Gardens into the distant mountains, 1940s

mountains primarily during the fall of the year, when he would collect ripe seeds for return to his father's botanical garden in Philadelphia. His legacy survives in the William Bartram Trail, which passes through the Appalachians well south of the Roan, skirting portions of North and South Carolina.

The Bartrams were instrumental in preparing the way for André Michaux, the true giant among the botanist-explorers in the southern Appalachians. Michaux was born near Versailles, France, in 1746. His wife died in childbirth in 1770, and after that he seemed to focus his attention on botany in an effort to overcome his grief. In 1785, the French government was looking to acquire plants and trees from eastern North America for its parks, and Michaux was commissioned for an expedition. His mission, in the words of his government, was "to make an intensive study of the trees and shrubs and to conduct such experiments as might be necessary to determine their fitness for transport to France."

He sailed to New York and the following year made it as far south as Charleston, South Carolina, where he organized his principal nursery. Michaux remained in North America until 1796. Among his important discoveries in the mountains of western North Carolina was the rare, beautiful plant called shortia. He also taught local settlers the value of ginseng and showed them how to prepare it for the market in China. From the point of view of a conservationist, it is a wonder that all of Michaux's collecting did not damage the integrity of mountain vegetation; in the fall of a single year, for example, he carried away more than twenty-five hundred trees, shrubs, and plant specimens from Burke and Yancey counties in North Carolina alone. In 1794, he explored the Roan and other peaks in the area, discovering several alpine species that had previously been observed only in Canada.

Toward the end of his time in North America, financial support from France started to wane, and Michaux began to feel like a forgotten man. He set sail for home from Charleston in 1796, his ship carrying a full array of his finest specimens. Michaux's first stroke of bad luck fell when the vessel wrecked off the coast of Holland. He fastened himself to a piece of plank and later washed ashore unconscious; his precious plants were saved, though they were saturated with salt water. Further disappointment awaited him when he arrived in Paris, as he discovered that only a small number of the six thousand specimens he had sent to France during his decade in North America were still surviving. The gardens of Paris, it seemed, had been among the victims of the French Revolution. Michaux recovered enough from the blow to return abroad in 1800, but he died of fever on the island of Madagascar two years later.

André Michaux left his mark on the world in his classic botanical guide, *Flora-Boreali Americana*. Within its pages are descriptions of the thousands of plant species he discovered, examined, and collected during his years of travel.

John Fraser, a Scotsman, was a noted botanist who explored the Roan in 1787, 1789, and 1799 under the patronage of the Russian government. Asa Gray, a botanist of a later generation, described the moment of one of Fraser's greatest discoveries on Roan Mountain: "On a spot which commands a view of five States, namely, Kentucky, Virginia, Tennessee, North Carolina and South Carolina, the eye ranging to a distance of seventy or eighty miles when the air is clear, it was Mr. Fraser's good fortune to discover and collect living specimens of the new and splendid *Rhododendron catawbiense*." Fraser is also credited with discovering the fir that now bears his name and stands as a remembrance of a man who considered the Roan one of his favorite botanizing locations.

Abies Fraseri, the Fraser fir, occurs naturally in areas of high rainfall above forty-five hundred feet in elevation, but it has lately been cultivated on plantations as low as fifteen hundred feet. The tree's beautiful shape, its dark green foliage, its strong branches, its pleasant aroma, and its excellent needle retention make it ideally suited for service as a Christmas tree. The Fraser fir's popularity has spawned an entire industry in the mountains.

A young Fraser fir under cultivation for use as a Christmas tree. The ones growing wild on the Roan will appear more gangly than this, as their branches are allowed to reach freely toward the sun.

There is a story that Fraser traveled for a time in the mountains with rival André Michaux. Michaux, it is said, feared that Fraser was dogging his footsteps so as to be certain not to miss out on any of the specimens Michaux intended to send to France. When he'd had his fill of Fraser's company, Michaux left him under the pretext of having to track down some horses that had strayed, and the two went their separate ways from that point onward. Such was the competitive spirit among botanists at that time. Fraser and his son returned to North America in 1807, and his son spent many years on the continent sending seeds and plants back to Great Britain after Fraser's death in 1811.

John Strother and the rest of the team that surveyed the Tennessee–North Carolina state line in 1799 were not botanists by trade, but they certainly were important figures in the early exploration of the Roan. Strother wrote of the hardships of travel in the mountains: "This day's march [up the Roan] was very severe, water scarce and that a considerable distance from the line. Had but an indifferent night's rest. The ground being very steep where we encamped was the cause of our resting but little. Add to this the severity of gnats." Strother was impressed with both the stiff wind and the view atop the Roan. "There is no shrubbage grows on the tops of this mountain for several miles, say, five," he wrote. "The wind has such a power on the top of this mountain that the ground is blowed in deep holes all over the northwest sides. The prospects from the Roan Mountain is more conspicuous than from any other part of the Appelatchin Mns."

Elisha Mitchell was a professor at the University of North Carolina in the days when that school boasted only three faculty members and ninety-odd students. Mitchell is most noted for his uncannily accurate measurements of the Black Mountains of North Carolina. He died in 1857 in a fall on the mountain later named in his honor; at 6,684 feet, Mount Mitchell is the highest peak east of the Black Hills of South Dakota. Professor Mitchell considered the Roan "the easiest of access and the most beautiful

The Rhododendron Gardens, with Roan High Bluff to the upper left

of all the high mountains" of the region. Of Roan Mountain's unique geography, he wrote,

> With the exception of a body of (granite) rocks, looking like the ruins of an old castle, near its southwestern extremity, the top of the Roan may be described as a vast meadow, (about nine miles in length, with some interruptions, and with a maximum elevation of six thousand and thirty eight feet,) without a tree to obstruct the prospect; where a person may gallop his horse for a mile or two, with Carolina at his feet on one side, and Tennessee on the other, and a green ocean of mountains raised into tremendous billows immediately about him. It is the pasture ground for the young horses of the whole country about it during the summer. We found the strawberry here in the greatest abundance and of the finest quality, in regard to both size and flavor, on the 30th of July.

The name of Harvard botanist Asa Gray is another familiar one throughout the area. Gray explored the Roan in 1840 and called it "without doubt, the most beautiful mountain east of the Rockies." Gray was born in Paris, New York, in 1810. He earned a medical degree but never used it, as his love of "the vegetable kingdom" pushed him instead toward a career in botany. His most famous article, "Notes on a Botanical Excursion into the Mountains of North Carolina," published in 1842, contained an impressive list of the plant species he discovered during his research. It was on the Roan that Gray found the lily he called *Lilium canadense*. With its deep red color and its throat speckled with black spots, it differed considerably from any lily previously known. Not long afterwards, Dr. Sereno Watson set it aside as a distinct species and

This panorama was probably even more sparsely vegetated when Elisha Mitchell boasted of galloping his horse along the crest of the Roan

renamed it *Lilium Grayi*, or Gray's lily, in honor of the man who discovered it. Gray's lily still blooms in the Rhododendron Gardens atop the Roan.

The mountain continued to attract scientists from all parts of the map through the latter stages of the nineteenth century. Describing the atmosphere of discovery on the Roan during the summer of 1880, J. W. Chickering noted that "an almost continuous scientific convention has been informally assembled on the summit." Early explorers in the area constituted a who's who of the botanical community, and the list of their findings is long and impressive.

If unusual plant species were responsible for bringing the first systematic explorations of Roan Mountain and the southern Appalachians, then timber and minerals were responsible for bringing industry to the region. Industry's interest in the mountains' timber actually predated interest in exploiting mineral resources, but major loggers were slow in pushing their way as far south and west as Roan Mountain, and it was after 1900 before the mills were operating in full swing. Logging and its effects on the land will be discussed more fully in a later chapter.

North Carolina has been called "the Specimen State" in mining circles. The title is a bit disparaging, since it implies that while the Tar Heel State is home to a great many kinds of minerals, few are present in great enough quantity to make exploiting them worthwhile. In the state's defense, it should be noted that iron, copper, mica, talc, kaolin, barite, corundum, and lime have all been discovered in paying quantities in North Carolina territory.

There are legends about ancient mining operations in the southern Appalachians. A tradition among the Indians of the region tells of white men on mules coming from the south during the summertime and carrying off a white metal with them. The legend probably contains a good measure of truth.

Thomas Lanier Clingman was an explorer, a congressman, and a key figure in the development of the North Carolina mountains

Gray's lily

throughout much of the nineteenth century. In 1867, Clingman discovered a small quantity of silver ore at the Sink Hole Mine, located just seven miles southwest of Bakersville, the closest community to Roan Mountain on the North Carolina side. Initial estimates suggested that the mine would yield about three hundred dollars' worth of silver per ton—a gross overestimate, as it turned out, but nonetheless the kind of promise that sets miners to digging with vigor. Clingman ordered a shaft to be sunk and two tunnels to be constructed but was disappointed to find nothing but mica.

Clingman and his men knew they were digging at an old mining site, but they were surprised when it came to light just how old the Sink Hole Mine really was. The Sink Hole site is a series of excavations sixty to eighty feet in diameter extending for about a third of a mile along a ridge. Old stone digging tools were found in some of the holes, and there was evidence of the use of metallic tools as well. More important, there were trees greater than three feet in diameter growing from some of the mounds of dirt removed in previous excavations. Clingman estimated that the timber rooted in the excavated earth was three hundred years of age, and in fact local resident Charles D. Stewart removed one such tree in 1872 and discovered that it contained three hundred rings in its trunk.

The revelations at the Sink Hole Mine lent credence to the theories that Spaniards in search of gold and silver explored the area way back in the sixteenth century. Hernando De Soto conducted an expedition in 1540, but he never made it as far north as the Roan Mountain area. Juan Pardo, who arrived in 1567, and the Spanish explorers of his generation are more likely candidates. Thus, there may have been significant interest in the area's mineral resources more than four centuries ago. But if there ever were notable deposits of silver around the Roan, then the Spaniards and their mules must have carted it all away.

It is interesting to note that Clingman and his men considered the mica they removed from the Sink Hole Mine to be worthless, simply discarding it as waste. A man named Heap stumbled upon Clingman's operation, took a block of mica with him over the mountains to Knoxville, Tennessee, and discovered that there was a market for it. He later returned with a partner, and the two of them successfully mined mica at the site for several years. In those days, mica was either pressed into sheets or ground, and it was used in such things as stoves, lamps, electrical machinery, insulation material, and wallpaper. Bits of the shiny, reflective material can still be found on the Sink Hole property.

The most important mine in the vicinity of the Roan is undoubtedly the Cranberry Mine, located in North Carolina just three miles off the Tennessee border on Cranberry Creek, named for the

The Cranberry Mine in the 1890s

abundant berries on its banks. Experts have called it one of the most remarkable iron deposits in the United States. The Cranberry vein actually stretches some twenty-two miles in a southwesterly direction, crossing the state line at Hump Mountain, at the northern end of the highlands of the Roan. In its day, it was a vein of remarkable purity, with high percentages of magnetic oxide of iron and metallic iron, but completely free of sulphur, the bane of the iron industry. The steep slopes at the Cranberry Mine were once covered with blocks of ore, many weighing hundreds of pounds. At times during the mining process, massive vertical walls of ore ten to fifteen feet thick were exposed. The main outcrop was fifteen hundred feet in length, ranging from two hundred to eight hundred feet in width.

There is an interesting story surrounding the discovery of the Cranberry vein. Three brothers from Crab Orchard, Tennessee—Joshua, Ben, and Jake Perkins—attended a logrolling near their home in 1826. They became involved in a scuffle with a man

A railroad on the Nolichucky River. The man standing near the tracks is believed to be General John T. Wilder.

named Wright Moreland and attempted to rob him of his clothes. After the incident, the incensed Moreland obtained warrants for their arrest. To avoid prosecution, the Perkins boys fled over the mountains to North Carolina, where they sought to support themselves by digging ginseng along the banks of Cranberry Creek. It was Joshua Perkins who found iron ore instead. The brothers were smart enough to take advantage of a North Carolina statute allowing anyone discovering ore on vacant land to construct a tilt-hammer forge; according to the statute, once the operators produced five thousand pounds of iron at their forge, the state would grant them three thousand acres at the site in an effort to encourage development. The Perkins boys were on their way.

Other miners staked their claims to portions of the deposit, and the Cranberry vein passed through a variety of owners—including General John T. Wilder, probably the most influential man in the development of Roan Mountain—during the remainder of the nineteenth century. It quickly became obvious that a modern transportation system was needed to ship the ore out of the mountains. Railroad companies were chartered for area service by the Tennessee General Assembly as early as 1866, but it was 1882 before the main line from Johnson City was opened. Production then skyrocketed. Between 1884 and 1893, about two hundred thousand tons of ore were mined at Cranberry. The ore was processed at a large blast furnace constructed in Johnson City, and the finished iron was then shipped to steel mills in Ohio and Pennsylvania to be used in the manufacture of high-quality steel. The railroad system built to exploit Cranberry's resources also opened the area for tourists, heralding Roan Mountain's heyday as a popular resort.

Operations at Cranberry were expanded during World War I, with annual production reaching sixty thousand tons. The facilities were closed during bad economic times in 1921, then opened again in 1923, then closed again in 1929. Some people say that the Great Depression didn't really come to the southern Appalachi-

ans; it was already there. By the time the stock market crashed, the
ore deposits at Cranberry had been largely depleted, the hillsides
had been stripped of timber, and flooding had become a dire
problem.

*Pegleg Mine, an offshoot of the Cranberry vein located
within Roan Mountain State Park*

Advertisements for the Cloudland Hotel claimed that the railroad trip to Roan Mountain was "beautiful beyond description, and far finer than anything else in the whole history of railroad engineering"

General Wilder on the Roan at age sixty-six

GENERAL JOHN T. WILDER

*J*ohn Thomas Wilder was an industrialist, an inventor, a Civil War hero, and an influential figure in the development of East Tennessee. He also stands as the single most important personage in the history of Roan Mountain. The Roan's glory days were Wilder's glory days.

Wilder was born in Hunter's Village in the Catskill Mountains of New York State on January 31, 1830. From his boyhood days, and without any formal training, he exhibited an avid interest in geology, collecting and arranging specimens in a small cabinet in his home. A restless soul, Wilder decided to head westward and try to make his fortune at the age of nineteen. He arrived in Columbus, Ohio, nearly penniless. An excerpt from the November 3, 1917, edition of the *Columbus Journal* bears testimony to the hardships of those early days, but also to the determined character that helped carry Wilder through: "One day while walking along Broad Street he espied a coin on the ground, which he seized and hastened to High Street to get a bun; but, when he reached the restaurant, he concluded that he would wait until he got hungrier before spending the coin, so he walked away with it in his pocket; and he kept that coin in his pocket through all of his eventful days."

Wilder did not go hungry for long. He landed employment at Ridgeway's Foundry, where he worked as an apprentice draftsman and pattern maker and was introduced to millwrighting. The owner of the foundry was so impressed with Wilder's talent and initiative that he offered to make him co-owner with his son upon his retirement if the two would operate the business together. Never lacking in confidence, Wilder declined the generous offer. He had bigger plans.

In 1857, he moved to Greensburg, Indiana, and opened his own modest foundry and millwrighting establishment. He married Martha Stewart, daughter of one of the town founders, shortly thereafter. In the years that followed, Wilder sold equipment and built mills and hydraulic works in the states of Indiana, Illinois, Wisconsin, Virginia, Kentucky, and Tennessee. He patented a turbine wheel and gained wide recognition as an expert in hydraulics. By the outbreak of the Civil War, his plant in Greensburg employed about a hundred men.

Wilder supported the Union cause, and he was determined to be part of the war effort. He closed his foundry, melted his metal down into bullets, raised a company of local men, and organized them into a light artillery company, the first three-year regiment recruited in Indiana. When it was determined that Wilder's artillery company did not fit into Union plans, the company was mustered into service with the Seventeenth Indiana Infantry, part of the Army of the Cumberland.

Within a month, Wilder was promoted from captain to the rank of lieutenant colonel without ever having been a major. His troops were eventually mounted on horseback and armed with Spencer Repeating Rifles. The news of their speed and toughness spread quickly, and they came to be known as Wilder's Lightning Brigade. Confederate cavalry leaders like Nathan Bedford Forrest, John Mosby, and Jeb Stuart held the advantage over their Federal counterparts early on, but as the war progressed and resources were exhausted, Union cavalry men like Phil Sheridan

Wilder by the Doe River

and Wilder more than held their own. Wilder and the Lightning Brigade earned respect from Union and Confederate forces alike, particularly distinguishing themselves in action at Chickamauga, Georgia, where they helped hold off victorious Confederate troops while the Union army retreated to Chattanooga. Wilder was made a brigadier general by the end of the war.

When the hostilities were over, Wilder resolved to move to Tennessee. There were a couple of reasons for the change. His health had suffered greatly during the war, and he hoped that a milder climate might do him good. And during his wartime forays into the Volunteer State, his entrepreneurial eye had been struck by the abundant natural resources waiting to be developed.

There is an amusing story surrounding Wilder's first ventures in the Chattanooga area shortly after his arrival in 1866. He was

Josie Pippin—a relative of Sherman Pippin, one of the hack drivers who brought guests up the mountain to the Cloudland Hotel—at her spinning wheel in the village of Roan Mountain

General Wilder looks on as two of his young relatives sit in a bowl carved from a single knot from one of the Roan's giant trees

This and other photographs from the General John T. Wilder Collection show scenes of Wilder's family on and around Roan Mountain

Wilder kin pose in what was known as "the Lyre Tree"

visiting the farm of a man he had fought alongside, Colonel Robert K. Byrd, and Byrd was trying to convince him that his farmland was highly suitable for development as a town site. "Colonel, what about the Emory River? Won't it flood these bottoms?" the skeptical Wilder purportedly asked. Byrd replied in the negative, but it was only a short time later that Wilder spied a small log lodged in a tree several feet off the ground. "Bob, what devilish boys put that log up that tree?" he promptly asked his companion. Wilder then proceeded to select another site near the Tennessee River ninety-two miles above Chattanooga. There, he discovered a four-foot-thick vein of iron ore, along with deposits of coal and iron that would be needed in the operation of a foundry. John Thomas Wilder was back in business.

In 1867, Wilder and two associates organized the Roane Iron Company, laid out and christened the town of Rockwood, and erected a blast furnace, the first using coke ever operated in the South. A second furnace was built nearby soon afterwards, and Wilder's reputation as an industrialist began to spread anew. He next concentrated his energies on Chattanooga and established the Roane Rolling Mills and Wilder's Machine Works, the former for the manufacture of railroad rails and the latter for the production of his patented turbine wheel. Sometime around 1870, he purchased seven thousand acres along the top and sides of Roan Mountain at a cost of $25.15 per acre. He also organized the Southern Car and Foundry Company, the Dayton Coal and Oil Company, and the Durham Coal Company, which operated on deposits found near the battlefield at Chickamauga, where he had once waged war.

Around the late 1870s, Wilder acquired a portion of the famous Cranberry Mine in North Carolina. The duke of Marlborough once visited Wilder in Johnson City and was treated to a tour of Cranberry. "General, how far downward does this vein of ore extend?" the duke inquired. "Your Grace," Wilder purportedly answered, "it is my opinion that the devil is now making iron from

The Wilder family in their front yard, with the Roan Mountain Inn in the background. Martha Stewart Wilder is in the rocking chair and General Wilder is third from the left.

the bottom of it." Industrial ventures toward the end of the general's career included the Carnegie Land Company in Johnson City and the Fentress Coal Company, located at the site of the present-day mining town that bears the name Wilder, appropriately enough.

It is important to draw a distinction between Wilder and the carpetbaggers of his generation, whose purpose it was to exploit whatever had value in a South in postwar turmoil. By contrast, Wilder gave more than he took. His first Tennessee furnaces were built at a time when the market was unstable, financial resources were limited, high interest rates were rampant, and technical knowledge was scant. His ventures were bold and risky, but not opportunistic. Wilder deserves a good share of credit for helping establish Chattanooga as an industrial center of the middle South.

His interests outside mining gave witness to his farsightedness and energy. While living in Johnson City, he served as vice-president of the Charleston, Cincinnati and Chicago Railroad, which later grew into the Carolina, Clinchfield and Ohio, one of the South's great coal carriers. Wilder also envisioned the development of Tennessee's water resources. He anticipated the Tennessee Valley Authority by more than twenty years when he helped organize a power company and acquired water rights along the Little Tennessee River; again, his role was that of pioneer, as others, not Wilder himself, profited from his vision in the years that followed.

He was less a success as a politician. Some said his forthrightness worked against him in that sphere. He was elected mayor of Chattanooga in 1871, only to resign eight months into his term. He was the Republican candidate for Congress from the Chattanooga district in 1876. He made up a large margin in the polls but ultimately lost. His judgment also failed him in his friendship with Alexander Graham Bell, as he declined the opportunity to invest in Bell's "toy" because he believed it would never amount to much.

The Wilders on their front porch in 1886. James A. Maher is on the left. Rachel Wilder Maher is at General Wilder's right knee and Edith Wilder Scott at his left knee.

Of greatest importance to Roan Mountain, Wilder built the Cloudland Hotel and opened the area to tourists from all points on the compass. He also constructed a home and a small hotel in the village of Roan Mountain. Built in the 1880s, the Roan Mountain Inn often served as a one-night stopover for people en route to the Cloudland Hotel, located on top of the mountain. The Roan Mountain Inn sat right on the Doe River, and its advertisements boasted that guests could catch fish off the back porch.

Interior views of the Wilder home

Samuel C. Williams, a former justice of the Tennessee Supreme
Court, effectively captured Wilder's appearance and personality
in a historical monograph published by Indiana University Press
in 1936:

> As to personal appearance: General Wilder was
> six feet two inches in height, but well propor-
> tioned. As age advanced he took on flesh but until
> after eighty years he moved with ease and a degree
> of grace. His eyes were particularly penetrating and
> bright; they were readily kindled by merriment. He
> had unusual conversational powers; his speech was
> spicy and at times emphasis was attempted to be
> lent by strong and explosive words, after the
> manner of many military men. His information was
> wide and in some directions ample, such as in the
> field of the history and traditions of the regions in
> which he resided, and in reminiscences of the great
> and near-great with whom he had come in contact.
> He was a total abstainer from intoxicants and made
> no use of tobacco; but at the board he was no mean
> trencherman, especially when confronting a juicy
> beefsteak.

Wilder's life was not a bed of roses. He lost a great deal of
money in the panic of 1893, and his finances never fully recovered. In fact, his losses cut so deeply that his daughter Edith was
forced to drop out of college. Edith Wilder recovered better than
did her father, as she went on to marry Arthur Hoyt Scott, who
played a part in the development of paper towels and tissues and
who helped bring the fledgling Scott Paper Company into the
international marketplace.

Despite his financial woes, General Wilder's popularity remained high. One of the most remarkable features about his life
was his surprising status among ex-Confederates and Southerners

The Wilder home in the village of Roan Mountain, listed on the National Register of Historic Places

in general. He became chairman of the Chickamauga National Park Commission, with responsibilities that included overseeing a site dedicated to the soldiers on both sides who met in one of the Civil War's great battles. He intervened to prevent the arrest and prosecution of former Confederate General Nathan Bedford Forrest on charges of parole violation, and he was later rewarded when the Nathan Bedford Forrest Post of the United Confederate Veterans made him an honorary member. During the Spanish-American War, Wilder traveled to Washington at his own expense to promote Knoxville as the site of a proposed training camp. That camp was christened Camp Wilder in his honor, and it became the home of the Sixth Tennessee Regiment. And in 1903, when a monument to Wilder's Lightning Brigade was to be dedicated, his old friends at the Nathan Bedford Forrest Post turned out as a body. As one of the post's members, Colonel Tomlinson Fort, said at the ceremony, "His name is a household word in the South; particularly in all East Tennessee, where he has lived continuously since the close of the war; and no man has done more than General Wilder in bringing order out of chaos."

The willingness to serve his country was something Wilder had in his blood. His was fifty-eight years of age at the outbreak of the Spanish-American War. When he learned that President McKinley was offering brigadier commissions to ex-Confederate Generals Fitzhugh Lee of Virginia and Joseph Wheeler of Alabama, he immediately sought service himself. Wilder subsequently learned that such appointments were being offered only to former Confederate generals, in acknowledgment that the South was sending tens of thousands of volunteers for the current war effort. He then tactfully backed off from his request.

Wilder died on October 20, 1917, in Jacksonville, Florida, where he had gone to avoid the rigorous fall and winter seasons native to his home of Monterey, Tennessee. An ex-Confederate delivered his funeral sermon. He was buried in Forest Hill Cemetery in Chattanooga.

CLOUDLAND

*I*t is not known exactly what motivated General John T. Wilder to build a resort hotel on a portion of the seven thousand acres he owned on Roan Mountain. Wilder himself had moved to Tennessee after the Civil War in an effort to improve his failing health, so perhaps he was hoping that other people with illnesses would come to partake of his cure. His resort eventually did become a haven for hay-fever sufferers.

The area atop the Roan was affectionately known as "Cloudland" among early visitors, in deference to the thick fogs and clouds that appeared out of nowhere to interrupt the view into the valleys below; the top of the mountain is actually shrouded about 75 percent of the time. The summit of Roan Mountain is also one of the few places in the world where a person can see his or her shadow in the clouds. To the people of Wilder's day, the name Cloudland bespoke excitement, surprise, a spirit of exploration, and a place where miracles happened. He adopted the name for his resort.

In 1877, under Wilder's direction, L. B. Searle constructed a twenty-room spruce-log structure on top of the Roan. It proved to be quite a summer haven for those who were tired of city life or just enjoyed the clean air of high elevations.

Clouds trapped among the distant peaks, referred to as "cloud lakes"

That first hotel was only a prelude, however. A larger structure was completed nearby in 1885 and formally named the Cloudland Hotel. A three-story frame structure at over 6,200 feet in elevation, it was quite possibly the highest human habitation east of the Rockies. Accounts of the number of rooms it contained varied from a little over 100 to a little less than 300; most estimates made the room count either 166 or 266. Everyone agreed on the number of bathrooms on the premises, though—there was only one!

The construction project must have been a monumental one, though the reported cost of forty thousand dollars seems a pittance by today's standards. The lack of public access to the site was one of the primary problems. Wilder and the others involved in the effort applied for and were granted permission to construct the first Carver's Gap Road, from Wilder's Forge on Big Rock Creek across the Roan to Carver's Gap and down the valley of Little

The original twenty-room spruce-log hotel on Roan Mountain

The Cloudland Hotel

Rock Creek to a ford near the home of John G. Burleson.

To hasten the building of the hotel, a steam sawmill was erected on the site so lumber could be sawed and planed locally. The majority of the structure was built of the balsam that grows on top of the mountain. Cherry was used for a good deal of the furniture, while hard maple cut to one-inch widths was shipped in to make a dance floor. The hotel was steam-heated, rather innovative for its day. Huge fireplaces were kept blazing most of the time, with the steam turned on when the temperature dropped at night. Water was supplied by a spring on the south side of the mountain some eight hundred feet below the top; hydraulic units lifted the water and deposited it in two storage tanks located at the rear of the hotel. The individual guest rooms boasted spring beds, copper bathtubs, and rugs.

There were facilities on the grounds for bowling, croquet, and golf. Pauline Stone, the daughter of N. L. Murrell, one of the hotel's operators, remembered the opening of the golf course this way: "My father took a club and ball and teed off for the first time and the ball made it from tee to green. The upshot of that was that they got special balls because the air at that altitude was such that any duffer could be a pro."

Within a year of the time the big hotel was completed, the first hotel and its surrounding buildings were burned to clear the area. A paved parking lot overlooking Tennessee now stands on the former site of the first hotel.

Once the Cloudland Hotel was in full operation, the main task was attracting enough guests to fill its many rooms. Cloudland's advertisements, like the one reproduced here, were models of mild overstatement. The emphasis, particularly with the testimonials that accompanied the descriptive copy, was on the health benefits of the Roan Mountain area, but the advertisements also touched on such minor matters as the welcome absence of insects, reptiles, and thunderbolts. Wilder understood that the local population could not provide the principal support for his hotel, so his ad

campaigns were directed at major American population centers
and even at the European market.

CLOUDLAND HOTEL,
Top of Roan Mountain,
6,394 FEET ABOVE THE SEA,
WESTERN NORTH CAROLINA,
ROAN MOUNTAIN HOTEL COMPANY,
PROPRIETORS.

*Address: ROAN MOUNTAIN HOTEL CO., Cloudland, Mitchell
Co., N.C.; or, ROAN MOUNTAIN HOTEL CO., Roan Mountain,
Carter Co., Tenn.—Daily Mails.*

PERFECT EXEMPTION FROM HAY FEVER.

COME UP OUT OF THE SULTRY PLAINS TO THE "LAND OF
THE SKY"—MAGNIFICENT VIEWS ABOVE THE CLOUDS
WHERE THE RIVERS ARE BORN—A MOST EXTENDED
PROSPECT OF 50,000 SQUARE MILES IN SEVEN DIFFER-
ENT STATES—ONE HUNDRED MOUNTAIN TOPS OVER
4,000 FEET HIGH, IN SIGHT.

DESCRIPTION.
CLOUDLAND HOTEL is situated on Roan Moun-
tain, Mitchell County, Western North Carolina,
twelve miles from Roan Mountain Station, on the
E. T. & W. N. C. R. R., which runs from Johnson
City on the East Tennessee Railroad, to Cranberry
Mines in North Carolina.

ROAN MOUNTAIN is an uplift in the heart of the
Western North Carolina Mountain system, overlooking the Unakas on the North and Blue Ridge
on the South. "It is," says Prof. Asa Gray, of Harvard College, "the most beautiful mountain east of
the Rockies." The mountain top is a beautiful
grassy prairie of 3,000 acres, dotted over with red

It has been suggested that the original hotel was torn down to make room for the grand one, but this rare view documents that they stood at the same time, if only for about a year. A log cabin was located between the two.

Rhododendrons, Azalias and Mountain Heather, in clumps from a yard to ten acres in area, set in the beautiful green sward, fringed with rich Balsams and Spruces, growing from beds of most luxuriant mosses. Here are deep woods, tangled thickets, wild glens and great cliffs of naked granite, hundreds of feet high, with deep, dense gorges beneath them whose stillness a human footfall has rarely broken. Thunder storms often fill the valleys while sunshine bathes the mountain top; and no grander view is ever seen than that presented on such an occasion. A hundred mountain peaks rise out of the storm clouds like islands in the sea, while lurid lightnings cleave the cloud lakes lying in the valleys below. The top of Roan Mountain being above dangerous lightning storm clouds, is free from thunder bolts. No insects or reptiles found at this altitude.

CLEAR COLD WATER, only thirteen degrees above freezing; beautiful brooks teeming with mountain trout, summer temperature from 48 to 73 degrees (usually 60 degrees); the most even temperature known—balmy, bracing air, its like can not be found by going North; a clean, healthful, pleasant, beautiful summer resort. Try it.

The hotel is the highest human habitation east of the Rocky Mountains, free from sudden changes.

The atmosphere is perfectly pure, and as a HEALTH RESORT, there can be no location more desirable. Consumption is unknown and malaria finds no refuge among these mountains.

PARTICULARS.

House open for the reception of guests, June 20th. Rhododendrons, Azalias, Heathers and Houstonias bloom in June. Most magnificent cloud views in September and October.

The hotel property and mountain are surrounded by a fence ten miles long entered by three gates. CAMPING ON THE MOUNTAIN IS NOT ALLOWED.

Board, $2.00 per day, $10.00 per week, $30.00 per month of four weeks.

Fires in private rooms, $5.00 per month for each room. Children under ten years, and servants, at half rates. Children occupying seats at first table to the exclusion of other guests, at full rates. We have no other family rates. Hack rates on extra baggage (all over 80 lbs.), $1.00 per hundred pounds.

Rooms neatly and comfortably furnished, floors carpeted, spring mattresses on all beds.

ROAN MOUNTAIN STATION HOTEL

Is new and well furnished. Rooms carpeted; good spring beds; thoroughly comfortable; and is 950 feet higher than any hotel on Lookout Mountain and 2,650 feet above sea level; a cool, restful resort. Cold water, cool nights. All at same rates as at Cloudland Hotel. It is on the railroad, with daily trains and W. U. Telegraph line. Good boating and fishing. Postoffice, Roan Mountain, Carter Co., Tenn.

HOW TO GET THERE.

Go by the East Tennessee system to Johnson City, and there take the Cranberry (Stem Winder) Narrow Guage Railroad to Roan Mountain Station, twenty-six miles from Johnson City, passing through Doe River Gorge, one of the wildest rides in the world. The Doe River Canyon is four miles long and 1,500 feet deep. Up this the railroad winds its way through four tunnels and over five bridges, in rocky clefts about 100 feet above the

river, through one of the most romantic spots on
the continent. The country along this line is beautiful beyond description, and far finer than anything else in the whole history of railroad engineering, alone fully repaying one for the time and
expense of the entire trip. At Roan Mountain
Station is a new, clean and well-furnished hotel,
owned by the company; also, a livery stable from
which a hack line runs to the top of Roan Mountain to Cloudland Hotel, a ride of twelve miles up
a new and beautiful road, winding up the sides of
the mountain, passing the most magnificent scenery at every turn, brings us to Cloudland Hotel on
top of the mountain, 6,394 feet above the sea.

A very interesting horseback or wagon ride can
be taken across the country from Marion, Round
Knob Hotel, Asheville, or Warm Springs, N. C., to
Roan Mountain, passing through the heart of the
Alleghenies, the finest mountain trip in any coun-
try.

SPECIAL EXCURSION RATES and coupon tick-
ets, good for the season, from all principal railroad
points. Covered hacks run from the railroad to the
mountain top; only reasonable fares charged. Eighty
pounds of baggage free.

TELEGRAPH AND EXPRESS OFFICES at Roan
Mountain Station.

TESTIMONIALS.
EXEMPTION FROM HAY FEVER.

Dr. D. B. Goodwin, of Pine Grove, Clark County, Ky., takes
pleasure in stating for the benefit of *Hay Cold Patients*, that he
has escaped his annual on Roan Mountain, N. C.

Mrs. Robt. Hereford Hare, of 2,031 DeLancey Place, Philadel-
phia, Penn., takes pleasure in stating for the benefit of *Hay Cold
Patients*, that during the ten years that she has suffered with *Hay
Fever*, she has sought and found relief by the seaside, at Caesar's
Head, at Mountain Lake and at the White Mountains, but no-

where in the United States has she found perfect exemption from the disease, until now at Cloudland Hotel on the top of Roan Mountain.

———————

816 F STREET, WASHINGTON, D. C., February 7, 1882.

Our party, without exception, were very greatly benefited by our summer on the Roan. I know of no summer vacation that has been of so great and permanent value to all of us as the one which we spent with you, and we certainly agree that none have been pleasanter.

My experience of two summers has created a most hearty desire for another visit in the near future, a wish shared by all our party.

WILLIAM B. KING.

———————

RENEWED BOUYANCY AND VITALITY.

HOUSE OF REPRESENTATIVES, WASHINGTON, D. C. Feb. 8, 1882.

I often recall with pleasure my sojourn at Cloudland last summer. The place needs only to be extensively known to be more liberally patronized. The mountain scenery is unsurpassed; I do not suppose there is a grander view east of the Rocky Mountains than that which is presented to the eye from Roan Bluff. The deliciously cool and invigorating mountain air seems to impart renewed bouyancy and vitality.

N. C. BLANCHARD, M. C. from Shreveport, La.

———————

CLIMATE CAN NOT BE EQUALED.

WASHINGTON, D. C., January 30, 1882.

I often think of the pleasant time I spent on Roan Mountain last summer. For beauty of scenery, cool and healthful climate, and freedom from summer's heat, I think it can not be equaled.

G. W. GRAY.

———————

ROAN MOUNTAIN CURED HER.

EATON, TENN., May 17, 1880.

My daughter was attacked in February, 1879, with pleuro-pneumonia, very badly, which resulted in complete hepatization of one lung, with an extensive effusion of serum and pus, which rendered it in this latitude, a hopeless case. But I am happy to say that she is entirely relieved, and was never in better health than now. I know that the trip to Roan Mountain cured her.

Respectfully, J. W. ROBINSON, M. D.

———————

LUNG AND THROAT TROUBLES.

DAYTON, OHIO, February 3, 1882.

Could I express my opinion of the Roan it would be a glowing description of, to me, the most beautiful spot on earth. No one could find a more healthful place, or more grand and beautiful scenery. Every minute on the Roan was full of pleasure and my health was much and permanently improved. Before going there I was greatly troubled with pain in my lungs, also with chronic sore throat; both of which almost entirely left me, and had I stayed until the close of the season, I believe I should have been perfectly restored. I feel that I was benefitted more than words can tell.

MRS. WILLIAM SHEPLER.

ASTHMA—SAVED HER LIFE.

PORT GIBSON, February 21, 1882.

My daughter, Nettie, sixteen years of age, suffered one year with a severe attack of the asthma, sleeping often in a chair. I tried many remedies and all to no avail. My physician finally recommended a change of climate. I accidentally saw in a railway guide that Roan Mountain was of high elevation; without a second thought I proceeded thither, and she had but one attack while on the Mountain, and that in the valley, at Bakersville. Since then she has attended to her studies and has been free from this dreadful and troublesome disease. I am of the opinion that her stay on the Mountain, roaming everywhere daily, wet or dry, in your invigorating climate, saved her life.

L. T. NEWMAN.

CHARLESTON, S. C., February 9, 1882.

I would so relish a draught of your glorious Mountain air. The dear old Roan and pleasant summer with you I remember with the very greatest pleasure, and am already planning to get up in June instead of July.

One small objection to the Roan is the inability to return to the lower world with comfort, however gradually we make the descent.

Don continues the hearty boy you did so much for last summer.

MRS. EDWIN P. FROST.

MUST BE FINANCIALLY INTERESTED.

12 DAUPHINE STREET, NEW ORLEANS, February 2, 1882.

I speak so constantly of Roan, its bracing air, splendid climate, etc., that my friends think I must be financially interested in Cloudland, and I am seriously thinking of asking you to certify that such is not the case.

C. EDMUND KELLS, JR., D. D. S.

WONDERFUL FLORAL DISPLAY.

PETERSBERG, N. Y., March 10, 1882.

I often think of my visit to Roan Mountain last June and of the wonderful floral display I there beheld in your beautiful Rhododendron Park. Truly the pure air, the delightful temperature, the clear, cold spring water, and the perfume-laden woodlands, make your "Land of the Sky" a veritable Arcadia.

C. W. REYNOLDS.

MAGNIFICENT ROAN MOUNTAIN.

NEW YORK CITY, N. Y., January 31, 1882.

It was my good pleasure to visit the magnificent Roan Mountain last June and behold the beauties of nature as viewed from this place 6394 feet above the level of the sea. To anyone in search of rest and quiet it is the SPOT. We arrived wearied with our long journey, and were thinking how old and tired we would be in the morning, but to our surprise, after a night of the sweetest sleep, we were feeling finely. I have traveled extensively but never found such pure and bracing air, and where one would recuperate so fast. I have seen the much admired prairie flowers but never saw anything equal to the beautiful wild flowers on Roan Mountain.

HENRY R. HARTSHORN.

THE HALF HAD NOT BEEN TOLD.

WILMINGTON, DELAWARE, February 3, 1882.

My recollections of Roan Mountain are of the most delightful kind. I would come and stay all summer with you if I could. Since my first visit in 1866 I have been three times on "The Roan." Before each of these visits I have feared that my recollections of its own beauty and of the grandeur of the views from it, might have caused me to be too enthusiastic in describing it to parties about to visit it for the first time, and that the result would be disappointment to them and to me. This has never occurred; all have confessed that the half had not been told them of this, the most beautiful of our mountains.

WM. M. CANBY.

Dr. Dan. C. Holliday, of New Orleans, in the *New Orleans Democrat*, says, writing under date of August 6, 1881: "Here we are at Cloudland, enjoying a temperature of morning 48 degrees, noon 65 degrees, night 48 to 52 degrees, and this only 48 hours from New Orleans! It appears really like fairy land."

The hotel's guest register is lost, so the list of luminaries who came to Roan Mountain will probably never be known. It *is* known that the governor of Louisiana, some European royalty, and Grafton Greene, a chief justice of the Tennessee Supreme Court and the man who would later write the court's opinion in the famous Scopes Monkey Trial, were among the guests.

The register also served as a kind of journal for the recording of the numerous plant species discovered on the mountain, so it would be of immense value to our knowledge of the early botany of the Roan. F. Lamson Scribner gave a hint of what the register might contain in an article published in the *Botanical Gazette* in 1889: "In the old register of the hotel are recorded the finds of the several botanists or botanical parties who have visited the locality. The first of these was made in 1878 by Dr. Geo. Vasey, who, under the head of 'Grasses of Roan Mountain,' enumerates the four or five species observed by him." Indeed, the register is considered such a treasure that, the better part of a century after Cloudland closed, history buffs still entertain hopes that it will one day be recovered from some forgotten, dusty attic.

The majority of visitors came not to list their botanical finds in the guest register, but rather for health reasons, as General Wilder might have envisioned. There is a remarkable tale of one young girl who had been flat on her back with severe asthma for most of her life. Her family heard tell of the Roan's remarkable curative powers and brought her there as a last resort. The girl lay on blankets and pillows in the back of an old buckboard as her driver started the slow climb up the winding road to Cloudland, but miraculously enough, she was up and sitting beside him by the time they reached the hotel. Such were the powers of the high mountain air. So many migrated to the Roan seeking relief from their allergies that they became known as "the Hay Fever Brigade." It is interesting to note that the hotel did not even open for the summer season until today's main attraction—the peak bloom period at the Rhododendron Gardens—had come and gone.

The view from Cloudland into North Carolina, "a boundless archipelago whose islands were the black peaks of the mountains"

Shots such as this one were put forth as photos of adventuresome hikers exploring the Roan, but they were actually staged. The road to the Cloudland Hotel ran right past Roan High Bluff. The hacks carrying visitors would stop and the people would disembark to pose for a professional photographer, then return to their hacks. The only actual hiking done on such occasions was to and from the waiting carriages.

Hikers posed on Roan High Bluff, formerly called Lion's Bluff

The ride up the mountain to Cloudland did not usually inspire such cures. In fact, it was by many accounts the most trying part of a vacation on the Roan. There is a story about Sherman Pippin, one of the men who drove their hacks from the railroad depot up to Cloudland. Pippin was meticulous enough to launder his blankets every day, which made his hack particularly popular among female visitors to the mountain. He was transporting a load of ladies up the road one terribly hot summer day when the conditions were so miserable that they all thought they would die of thirst. It just so happened that Pippin was also carrying a cask of whiskey destined for the hotel bar, so he took a penknife, bored a hole in the barrel, distributed good cheer to all present, and cut a plug to fit the hole. His patrons arrived at Cloudland well satisfied, and the barkeeper was never the wiser.

Once they reached the top of the mountain, most Cloudland guests commented favorably on the mild weather, the variety of the plant life present, and the quality of the air. In *The Heart of the Alleghanies*, Wilbur G. Zeigler and Ben S. Grosscup wrote eloquently of the view from Roan Mountain:

> While I was at the hotel a terrific thunder storm visited—not the summit of the Roan—but the valleys below it. It came after dark, and from the porch we looked out and down upon the world in which it raged. Every flash of lightning was a revelation of glory, disclosing a sea of clouds of immaculate whiteness—a boundless archipelago whose islands were the black peaks of the mountains. Not a valley could be seen; nothing but the snowy bosom of this cloud ocean, and the stately summits which had lifted themselves above its vapors. In the height of the storm, the lightning blazed in one incessant sheet, and the thunder came rolling up through the black awful edge of the balsams, producing somewhat similar sensations to those which fill the breast of a superstitious savage at the recurrence of an every-day storm above him.

Noted mountain traveler Charles Dudley Warner visited Cloudland in 1885. "The hotel," he remembered, "provided two comfortable rooms for office and a sitting room with partitioned off sleeping places in the loft. It set a good table, but rocked like a ship at sea when the wind blew."

The fees charged at Cloudland come as something of a shock. Guests could rent a room for $2 per day, $10 per week, or $30 for four weeks. If they wanted a room with a fireplace, they had to pay $5 per month extra. Cloudland's prices seem so low that the *Johnson City Press-Chronicle* was moved to publish a wistful article called "What this country needs is a good $2 hotel" back in the spring of 1970. The article told the story of how an Illinois man, Julian P. How, had unearthed one of Cloudland's old advertising brochures among his father's papers. How's imagination was captured by both the flowery wording of the advertisement and the wonderful place it described, so he put the brochure in an envelope, addressed it to "The Proprietor, The Roan Mountain Hotel, Carter County, Roan Mountain," and jokingly inquired as to whether a room could still be had at the quoted price. Just as he anticipated, the answer came back that the rates were no longer in effect, and that the Cloudland Hotel had in fact passed from existence.

Two dollars bought a lot before the turn of the century. Cloudland kept a doctor, a butcher, a baker, and a barber in residence. The property was surrounded by a fence ten miles long, entered by three separate gates. A post office was eventually set up in the hotel, with mail addressed to Cloudland, North Carolina; it was possible to have mail delivered in winter, though it sometimes took an industrious person to make it to the top of the mountain.

Waitresses at the Cloudland Hotel were assigned eight tables each. Their pay was twelve dollars a month plus tips. Room-service meals to elderly patrons sometimes brought five-dollar tips.

The guests did not go hungry. Flour, sugar, and other bulk staples were hauled up the mountain by wagon, while items like vegetables, eggs, and fresh fruit were often carried on horseback. Food that was prone to spoiling was kept in a house above a spring whose water was, as Cloudland's advertisements liked to boast, "only thirteen degrees above freezing." Breakfast always consisted of bacon, liver, steak, fried apples, fried potatoes, flannel cakes, biscuits, coffee, and eggs. The main meal was served at midday, with a choice of two soups, two meat entrées—perhaps one of them the juicy beefsteak so favored by General Wilder— six vegetables, and a selection of four desserts. Supper was a bit lighter, with cereal, meats, eggs, flannel cakes, and portions left over from the midday menu. Musical entertainment accompanied the evening meal as an aid to digestion.

One of the most notable facts about Cloudland was that, like the

The Cloudland Hotel in its heyday

ridge line of Roan Mountain itself, the hotel straddled the Tennessee–North Carolina boundary. Guests could sleep in one state and dine in the other. The hotel drew the maximum effect from its geography, even going so far as to paint a white line through the dining room and down the length of the long banquet table, with the names of North Carolina and Tennessee painted on their appropriate sides. The demarcation was done mainly in jest, but it had its practical side, too: drinking alcoholic beverages was legal in Tennessee but illegal in North Carolina, so guests needed to be certain where they stood when they imbibed. It was said that the local sheriff from North Carolina spent many an idle hour at Cloudland waiting for someone to slip up and become a new customer for his jail.

Visitors enjoyed the novel geography and the atmosphere of merriment. They liked to sit on the wide porches running the length of the south and east sides of the hotel and watch the sun bathe the mountaintop. But even the Cloudland Hotel could not conquer human nature—that is to say, it couldn't please everyone. One guest who left Roan Mountain with decidedly mixed feelings was Henry T. Finck, a New York music critic who wielded an acerbic pen. The source of Finck's dissatisfaction was a song called "A Hot Time in the Old Town," as revealed in an article he wrote for the *Brooklyn Citizen* in 1900. Perhaps Cloudland should not bear the blame for a guest who arrived on the Roan already bearing excess baggage. Finck's elaborate complaint went as follows:

> One afternoon, when I was watering flowers in the backyard, a boy in the street whistled a tune that I had not heard before. Had he been within reach I should certainly have turned the hose on him, for the infliction of that tune on my unwilling ears seemed as great an outrage as if he had thrown a rotten potato in my face. It made me, to use a colloquial phrase, "mad as a hornet," not only because of its

offensive vulgarity, but because there was something
in the nature of that mephitic air that made me feel
certain I should hear it a thousand times during the
summer. And by prophetic soul divined the truth. In
the course of a week or two every boy in town was
whistling that tune, every other man humming it, and
every tenth woman playing it on the piano. I fled
from New York and buried myself in the Mammoth
Cave in Kentucky. In course of the ten-hour trip, a
young man in our party whistled that tune half a
dozen times, amid the sublimities of subterranean
rivers, vaulting domes, and bottomless abysses. I
went to the highest habitation east of the Rocky
Mountains, the Cloudland Hotel, on the border of
North Carolina and Tennessee. For several days there
was peace, and life once more seemed worth living;
but ere long a young woman arrived to take charge of
the piano, and every other piece she played was an
arrangement of that detestable song. I changed my
room from North Carolina to the wing in Tennessee,
plugged my ears with wax, and continued my literary
task. In September I went to the mountains of Maine
and took a room in a farmhouse. There was a cottage
opposite, with a piano and a young lady, and—but
why continue this harrassing [sic] tale? The song, I
may add, was "A Hot Time in the Old Town," which
May Irwin, I believe, was the first to perpetrate in
this country, though I don't pretend to be an expert
in criminal history.

What is there in the nature of that song that made
it thus ravage the country like an epidemic from East
to West, from South to North? In other words, what
makes a vulgar song popular or gives a popular song
its circulation? Or, to put the question in a still more
comprehensive form, How can we account for the
surprising vogue of certain songs and pieces that are
not a bit better than a thousand others of their class
not successful, and vastly inferior to many gems of
the great masters that are neglected except by the
chosen few?

The Cloudland and a portion of its ten-mile fence. Roan High Knob can be seen to the right.

It is a pity that Cloudland's register is lost, because we can probably never know whether Henry T. Finck ever returned to Roan Mountain in a better frame of mind.

Cloudland's light may have been bright, but it burned out rather quickly. Even the patronage of European royalty could not support what must have been a very expensive operation. Paul Fink, author of *Backpacking Was the Only Way*, noted that Cloudland "was never a great financial success," and it is easy to guess why. The cost of shipping in foodstuffs and other products was high. The vacation season in the mountains was short—not much more than ninety days—yet the building had to be maintained year-round. Fires had to be burned all night ever during the summertime. The skeleton staff that remained through the winter could attest to the harsh conditions—mail deliveries often had to be passed through the windows, as the snow sometimes drifted so high that the doors were entirely blocked, and even when that was not the case, the wind might be blowing so hard that the doors could not be pushed open against it. Anyone who has spent much time on the Roan knows the kind of wear and tear that is caused by the wind. Upkeep on the hotel must have been enormous.

General Wilder was the moving force behind Cloudland, and perhaps the most telling factor in the hotel's decline was his decision to turn his boundless energy to other projects and leave the day-to-day operations on the top of the Roan in the hands of others. Cloudland passed through several managers, who ran it in accordance with lease agreements. The first of them was Frank Stratton. Next came W. E. Ragsdale of Chattanooga, and then N. L. Murrell and a man named Wagoner, who operated the hotel in partnership for a time.

Murrell was the last to run Cloudland under lease. In fact, as Murrell's daughter, Pauline Stone, reported, General Wilder "offered him the hotel at Cloudland and considerable acreage for $20,000, nothing down and pay for it as he could. My father did not take it." Running Cloudland was a family affair for the

Murrells. Mrs. Murrell was still speaking fondly of the experience when she was well into her eighties. When a newspaper reporter once asked her what kind of dancing was practiced at the hotel in the old days, she replied spiritedly, "Why my dear, it wasn't the Dark Ages. We waltzed, enjoyed square and ballroom dancing." While she grudgingly admitted that Mount Mitchell was higher than the Roan, she took special pride in pointing out that "it was not inhabited."

After N. L. Murrell's lease ran out, Cloudland passed into the hands of John Gouge, an old-timer who had helped build Wilder's original twenty-room structure on Roan Mountain. Gouge was employed as caretaker, and his salary was forty dollars per year plus whatever profit he could turn from summer guests. General Wilder was still sending money to be used for the repair and maintenance of the building in those days, but some say that his caretaker preferred to spend it on other indulgences. Whatever the case, Cloudland was headed downhill after the turn of the century and was finally abandoned sometime around 1910. Local people would come in to ransack the remains, throwing fragile objects from the windows and breaking them to pieces. Paul Fink passed through the area on one of his backpacking trips in 1915 and noted that "the ravages of wind and weather were already evident— glassless windows, leaking roofs, sagging floors and a general atmosphere of decay."

Wilder eventually sold the remnants of his paradise to a man from Burbank, Tennessee, who in turn sold off what was left of the hotel room by room. People would arrange to purchase one or more rooms and then take whatever they could find—basically, the lumber, door, and window frames. For years afterward, it was not unusual to find homes and businesses in the area built entirely from Cloudland lumber. On rare occasions, people used their hotel room's door—complete with room number—as the front door to their residence. I once happened upon an abandoned house constructed of Cloudland lumber when I was out hiking. It felt like

Cloudland beginning to show signs of disrepair. Note the collapsed condition of the porch and the fence.

I was stepping back to the days just following the hotel's closing, as the furnishings and possessions of the long-departed inhabitants—cast-iron stove, canned food on the shelves, clothing hanging in place, corn-shuck mattresses—were completely intact, as if the owners would return at any minute.

Cloudland's fine furniture was scattered throughout Tennessee and North Carolina, but such items as washstands, trunks, dressers, and beautiful hand-pegged cherry beds become available only rarely today. Collectors have long since located and bought what they could, while other pieces remain in the possession of the families that have held them through the years.

I once visited the home of a fascinating gentleman who had spent the first twelve years of his life in the Cloudland Hotel, as his parents were employed there. He told me many wonderful tales of his experiences on top of the Roan, but what I found especially interesting was his account of what had become of the hundred or two hundred rooms full of furniture. It was his parents, he said, who at the closing of the hotel had brought down much of the furniture and distributed it among their neighbors and friends.

The famous banquet table immediately came to mind, and I asked whether he knew what had happened to it. "Oh, that," he responded. "It's right here in the kitchen. Would you like to see it?" My heart nearly dropped, as I'd long assumed that the table had been destroyed. We went into the kitchen and there before me was a narrow, six-foot-long table with pale green planks for its top, and with that legendary white line painted right down the center. But it was so short! How could that tiny table possibly have accommodated all the guests at the Cloudland Hotel? If a six-foot table could be exaggerated to grand proportions, then how accurate were all the other stories I'd heard about the hotel? My host was quick to dispel my doubts. He said the table had been so big that he couldn't hope to fit it into his house, so he had cut it down to its present size and burned the rest as firewood! I was both relieved that the table had once been as big as reported and

Rubble from the Cloudland Hotel in 1927. Roan High Knob is in the background.

disappointed that most of it had gone up in smoke.

With both the Cloudland Hotel and Roan Mountain, it is sometimes difficult to tell where fact ends and legend begins. One
prominent local legend concerns the so-called mountain music of
the Roan. The story is an old one. Herdsmen in the area occasion-
ally heard a strange sound when the wind blew. Some judged it to
be perfectly natural, merely the amplification of normal wind
noises caused by the configuration of rocks on the Roan. Others
offered more colorful explanations. One story that arose claimed
that the mountain was actually talking. Another said that it was the
devil's wind that set clouds to whirling around the mountain in a
circular pattern and caused the eerie sound. Still another took the
completely opposite approach and ascribed the noise to angels
singing in the air over the Roan, perhaps even practicing for
Judgment Day; according to that version, the mountain was
blessed. It was said that mountain music could only be heard when
the air at the peak was clear and the sky blue, but thunderstorms
raged in the valleys below.

The legend was still kicking around in the days when General
Wilder's twenty-room log structure stood atop the Roan, but the
popular view by then was that mountain music sounded like the
buzzing of a thick swarm of bees. In 1878, Knoxville scientist
Henry E. Colton traveled to Roan Mountain to witness the phenomenon. He happened to be present on a night when the sound
was particularly loud. General Wilder had often heard and spoken
of mountain music himself, and he and two other men accompanied Colton out onto the mountain that evening. Colton subsequently returned home and wrote an account of his experience for
a Knoxville newspaper. Like many of the scientific explanations
that attempted to account for the origin of the balds, Colton's
article was a model of convoluted thinking:

> The sound was very plain to the ear, and was not
> at all as described—like the humming of thousands

of bees—but like the incessant, continuous and
combined snap of two Leyden jars [devices for storing
electrical charges] positively and negatively charged. I
tried to account for it on the theory of bees or flies but
the mountain people said it frequently occurred after
the bees or flies had gone to their winter homes or
before they came out. It was always loudest and most
prolonged just before there would be a thunderstorm in
either valley, or one passing over the mountain. I used
every argument I could to persuade myself that it was
simply a result of some common cause and to shake
the faith of the country people in its mysterious origin
but I only convinced myself that it was the result from
two currents of air meeting each other in the suck
between the two peaks where there was no obstruction
of trees, one containing a greater, the other a less
amount of electricity, or that the two currents coming
together in the open plateau on the high elevation, by
their friction and being of different temperatures,
generated electricity. The "mountain music" was
simply the snapping caused by this friction and this
generation of electricity.

Perhaps we should be thankful that the scientific community
never pursued the question of mountain music as vigorously as it
did explanations of the balds.

Some people deny the existence of mountain music altogether.
One correspondent of mine who now lives in the desert Southwest
claims that neither she nor her family heard the noise during their
many years on the Roan. If others have heard it, she suspects they
were merely witnessing the same sort of sound she has heard in the
desert when the wind sings through the wire fences that surround
many ranches—an interesting noise, perhaps, but hardly a fitting
subject for legend and mystery. Still, a good many of the old-
timers I spoke with were confident in remembering strains of
mountain music from the days of their youth.

Another well-known Roan Mountain legend is loosely tied to

mountain music, or to the conditions that bring on mountain music, at least. When the valley storms associated with the buzzing or snapping sound eventually clear away, it is said that people standing high on the mountain can look down upon a rainbow that forms a complete circle. Legend has it that the rainbow is God's halo, or a halo left by God's angels to protect the Roan and its visitors from all that is evil.

Witnesses to the circular rainbow are harder to come by than are people who have heard mountain music. In fact, I had such bad luck locating *anyone* who had seen the rainbow that I was skeptical of the legend, until one particularly blustery day when I was planning a full-moon hike to the highlands of the Roan for a group of visitors to the state park. Close to fifty people had signed up for the trip, so needless to say I grew quite concerned when thick storm clouds rolled in and completely covered the top of the mountain that afternoon. Since I didn't want to lead the group into a torrent of rain later that night, I decided I ought to make an early

A rainbow over the Roan. View from the Rhododendron Gardens toward Roan High Knob.

jaunt to the top and check out the conditions there.

As I drove up the mountainside with a friend, the fog grew thicker and thicker. Convinced that the weather was not going to give way, I was about to turn back and cancel the hike when the cloud cover abruptly fell away. It seemed as if the whole world had opened up before us. We found ourselves under clear blue skies with the storms rolling below us in the valleys. Then, looking to the right, I saw the most unbelievable phenomenon I have ever witnessed. A rainbow began to materialize at eye level, and as it developed it took the form of a complete circle. And then a *second* rainbow formed within the circle of the first! I can't say how long we stood there. It seemed like a short eternity before the elusive rainbow faded from view. I reaffirmed my faith in legends on the spot.

It is not known whether General Wilder or any of his guests on Roan Mountain ever witnessed the circular rainbow. The general and some of the others *did* hear mountain music. All things being equal, it would figure to be easier to witness mountain music today than it was in Wilder's time, since things are considerably quieter on top of the Roan now than they were during the heyday of the Cloudland Hotel.

All that remains of Cloudland is the stone foundation. Spruce and fir trees grow among the ruins. Yet with a good imagination, you can walk through the kitchen, rock on one of the porches, straddle the state line, or dance in the main hall. You can almost hear the music that once echoed from the Cloudland Hotel across the surrounding highlands. Though the building has nearly disappeared, a visit to the site will convince you that its spirit still lives.

$\mathcal{T}$he forests on Roan Mountain once boasted a grandeur seldom, if ever, seen today. As recently as the 1880s, botanists were still attesting to a level of growth that seems difficult to believe. "It was not uncommon to find logs whose diameter was nearly five feet," E. G. Britton wrote in 1886. "Between 3,000 or 4,000 feet of altitude," J. W. Chickering noted in 1880, "we notice the enormous chestnuts, *Castanea visca*, one measuring 24 feet in circumference and hundreds of others five and seven feet around and running seventy or eighty feet without a limb." Chickering wrote elsewhere that "one specimen of *Prunus serotina* [black cherry] was measured, which was 19 feet in circumference and probably 70 feet without a limb and straight as a pine."

For one reason or another, the Roan's trees have been felled since the early days of settlement. The kind of mighty specimens seen by the likes of Britton and Chickering have long passed from existence. The hardships of living back in the hills and hollows of Roan Mountain in times gone by were many. Travel was difficult. Winter weather was harsh. Survival was a daily task undertaken by all the members of a family. Crops had to be grown, money had to be raised, and livestock had to be fed. Settlers' efforts at meeting those goals brought a great deal of suffering upon the forests and the land itself.

Farmland was first cleared in the bottoms, then successively higher and higher up the ridges. Trees were killed by girdling, thus eliminating unwanted shade and invading root systems. Most trees were left to fall before being rolled into heaps and burned. Settlers also burned woodland to create pasturage—a process known as "greening the grass"—and they turned their cattle and pigs loose on the forests, leading to the trampling of countless young trees.

The soil on Roan Mountain and in the surrounding area was uncommonly rich. It boasted a layer of humus several inches thick above a base that was black and porous, thanks to the large percentage of decayed vegetable matter it contained. But the effects of being exposed to sun and rain were devastating, and the soil was quickly depleted and eroded upon being cultivated. Once the humus layer was carried away, the soil lost much of its capacity for holding water, and when soil cannot hold water, it is ripe for further erosion. Rainfall of eight inches in the span of eleven hours has been recorded in the Roan Mountain area. Such a quantity of water will have an impact on any kind of terrain, but that impact is most pronounced on steep, bare slopes. As a 1902 Department of Agriculture report on conditions in the southern Appalachian region stated,

> The effect of exposing mountain lands to the full power of rain, running water, and frost is not generally appreciated. The greater part of our population lives on level land and does not see how the hills erode, and even in the hills nearly all the people go indoors when it rains and therefore do not half understand what is going on. In the dashing, cutting rains of these mountains the earth of freshly burned or freshly plowed land melts away like sugar. The streams from such lands are often more than half earth and the amount of best soil thus eroded every year is enormous.

Thelma Brown, wife of Dr. D. M. Brown, and grazing sheep on Round Bald. Grassy Ridge Bald is in the background.

The first year after clearing, most mountain fields were planted in corn or buckwheat. One or two more years of cultivation in corn followed, then a year or two of wheat, rye, or oats, and then the fields went to grass. It wasn't long before weeds and gullies took the fields and destroyed their worth. More and more fields had to be cleared to replace those that had died so quickly. And the forests had a difficult, if not impossible, time reestablishing themselves on the depleted soil.

Settlers used their timber to supplement the difficult living they made from farming. They turned a fair profit by selling cherry, black walnut, hickory, and tulip poplar for fuel and fencing, but they further harmed the land in the process. They tended to fell trees wastefully high on the stump, and they gave little consideration to cutting them in the direction where they would do the least damage in crushing younger trees. In retrospect, it was also shortsighted that they cut black walnut and other prime species for use in fencing and the like simply because oak and pine were not so close at hand. In fairness, though, early settlers could not be expected to be fully aware of the consequences of their land management, and the damage they caused was nothing in comparison with what followed when commercial lumbering firms moved into the area.

The difficult access to the forests of the southern Appalachians meant that lumber companies were rather slow in exploiting them. Naval stores were produced from the pine forests of colonial North Carolina, but big-time logging in the United States really began in Maine and the rest of New England. It was the development of the steam-powered circular saw in the 1820s that made the move westward and southward possible. After the hardwood stock in Pennsylvania, Ohio, Indiana, and Illinois was picked over, timber scouts made their way to the southern Appalachians. They were looking for cabinet woods like walnut, cherry, birch, ash, and hickory, and they also hoped to find construction timber like tulip poplar, white pine, and basswood. Caleb Trentham set up a

Loggers on the Roan

sawmill on the Little Pigeon River near Gatlinburg, Tennessee, in 1868, and other firms followed soon afterward. Logging practices were fairly conservative in the early days. Timber was cut selectively, as mills did not want logs less than twenty inches thick at the small end. Few fires were built in the forests, and natural reproduction was not interrupted.

Roan Mountain was ripe for exploitation. It is believed that approximately three million board feet of cherry were shipped to the mills via Engine Gap, the low area between Round Bald and Jane Bald. The transportation system used at Engine Gap was an ingenious one. An incline railway was constructed through the gap from Burbank, Tennessee, to Roan Valley in North Carolina. That arrangement was unusual, as timber is customarily funneled *down* a mountain, not *up* it. There was a wire running from the Tennessee side up the Roan to Engine Gap, where a bell was tied. When lumber collected in the Volunteer State was ready for

Water wheel at a local sawmill

Boy perched atop the flume that ran down the mountain from Burbank

shipment, the bell was rung, and the operator of the stationary steam engine located at Engine Gap set about pulling the load up the mountain and sending it over the top and down to the mills in North Carolina.

There were other logging operations in the area, too. Up and down the hills and hollows, water wheels were set up to power sawmills, and flumes were constructed to move cut timber from higher to lower elevations. The flume system, in which water running through a long chute helped propel the logs downhill, was certainly more practical than dragging timber up a mountain.

One of the more talked-about flumes in the area ran from Burbank, just above the current site of Roan Mountain State Park, down to the village of Roan Mountain. Local residents liked to use the flume for many pastimes outside the realm of lumbering. Walking the high beams of the structure was popular among young and old alike. One man, remembering his boyhood days, remarked, "We used to walk clear from Burbank to town on top of the flume. I remember folks a-floatin' all kinds of stuff down it, too. They'd float pigs and chickens and whatever else they could get their hands on. Once someone nailed a duck by its feet to an old board and sent it down."

Another fellow recounted a wild and woolly tale that is hard to believe, though he swore it was the truth. It seems that while cutting timber above Burbank during the winter, some pour soul was killed when a tree fell on him. "The snow was too deep to ever get him down to the village for a decent burial," my source said, "so he was wrapped up real good and put in the flume. When he popped out the other end he was tended to proper-like." The reaction of the men at the bottom end of the flume is difficult to guess, especially if they knew the victim but hadn't heard of his passing. When the flume from Burbank to the village of Roan Mountain was torn down, its lumber was used by local residents in the building of barns, boxes, and the like.

Early logging efforts, even though they were considerably

A 1902 view of erosion on Roan Mountain

smaller in scope than those that followed, were a prelude to disaster. There were indications that trouble was coming. Scattered here and there on the steep slopes of the southern Appalachians was evidence of landslides in times of heavy rainfall, evidence that whole sections of forest had been uprooted and sent downhill, only to be stopped yards later by stands of trees on firmer footing. And many of those instances were in virgin forest, where the humus layer was deep and the soil was in excellent condition. The potential for landslides was infinitely greater where lumbering had taken place.

In 1901, from May 20 to May 23, the southern Appalachians saw rain and floodwater unlike any in memory. The people who lived though it christened it "the May Flood," and for years afterward they told tales of pigs and cattle washing away, of neighbors going downstream on the roofs of their homes, never to be seen again, and of everything communities and families had worked for being totally destroyed. The losses associated with the flood were incredible. Along the Catawba River, farmland was swept away for more than two hundred miles. Erosion was so severe that it was reported that *all* the soil in many creeks had been removed, leaving only large stones and rocks. Almost all the dwellings and farms in the flood plain were destroyed, along with railroad bridges, roadbeds, and culverts. Mountains of lumber from destroyed buildings in Mitchell County, North Carolina, were found on the Nolichucky River near Greeneville, Tennessee.

In the vicinity of Roan Mountain, the private narrow-gauge railroad of the Forge Mining Company was devastated, its track washed out in thirty-nine places. All the bridges in the Doe River Gorge were destroyed. Damage was so great within the confines of the gorge that train service was not restored until August.

A letter from James A. Maher to General Wilder, his father-in-law, contains one of the best accounts of the flood scene. Maher

A small landslide stopped by the forest on the north slope of the Roan

Debris from the May Flood along the Nolichucky River

and his wife, Rachel, were in Knoxville visiting the sick General Wilder when the waters came. Anxious for news about their children, who had remained at their house in the village of Roan Mountain, the Mahers traveled to Johnson City, then hired a hack to take them home. The hack could make it no farther than two miles above Hampton, at which time the Mahers continued on horseback. They finally completed the journey on foot. Maher described the flood's aftermath for General Wilder soon upon arriving home:

It began raining again last night and is still raining steadily. The people all along the way and here especially are panic stricken, and the rain frightens them. If you could see the place, or what was the place, you would not wonder. Men, women and children were overjoyed to see us and they hung around Rachel like a savior. I cannot enumerate the damages in a letter. Of course we are damaged three times more than the rest of the town combined, but the loss of the poor people is complete and absolute and their condition is pitiful. . . . You can believe no one, as no man appears to have been a quarter of a mile from his home, and there are lots of wild rumors, all garnished in the telling.

The north side of the town, between the river and the railroad and below the hotel [the Roan Mountain Inn], is a rocky waste, covered with pools—it is all irretrievably gone. The lower meadow, or where the lower meadow was, is in the same condition—a shining, rocky waste. . . . You cannot imagine the desolate look of things. The river covered the valley from mountain to mountain—gorged below and scoured the rocks bare of soil. The house is uninjured—the only one unhurt in the place. One-third of the river now flows through the upper meadow and between the house and the mill. There is not a garden left in this valley.

To make matters worse, the summer of 1902 produced floodwaters comparable to those of the May Flood. Damages were estimated at more than ten million dollars, a staggering figure in those days. It was obvious that something had to be done. The Department of Agriculture examined the situation and generated an inch-thick report on conditions in the southern Appalachians, a portion of which was quoted earlier in this chapter. The report documented harmful farming practices, fires, clearcutting, landslides, and erosion problems—all perpetrated in the name of short-term self-interest, whether by landowners or lumbering concerns. The investigators' conclusion was sobering: "While the damage from the storm of 1901 exceeds that of any preceding year, it is common knowledge among the mountaineers that annually the floods have risen irregularly but steadily higher, and that their destructive work has been increasing in proportion as the forest clearings and forest burnings have proceeded. We may confidently expect that floods of the future will exceed those of the past."

The report went on to recommend the establishment of a national park in the southern Appalachians. It was not the first time the idea had been proposed, but the movement started to gather momentum after the floods of 1901 and 1902. Still, it was eight more years before legislation was passed to just *begin* the purchase of federal parkland in the eastern part of the country. The Weeks Act appropriated ten million dollars "for the purchase of wild lands in the mountains at the heads of navigable rivers of the Eastern United States." The money was spread among several states. Roan Mountain, along with numerous other sites, was proposed as the location for the park in the southern Appalachians, but the land finally decided upon was a tract due west of Asheville, North Carolina. It boasted one of the last primeval forests east of the Mississippi.

The closest national park in those days was Yellowstone, two thousand miles away. Like the other parks in the West, Yellowstone was built on land already owned by the federal government. Conditions were different in the eastern United States. The good news was that mountain land could be had at around two dollars per acre. The bad news with the land selected for Great Smoky Mountains National Park was that it had to be acquired entirely from private owners in no fewer than sixty-six hundred separate tracts. The task was a monumental one, and it was 1940 before President Franklin D. Roosevelt finally dedicated the park. Great Smoky Mountains National Park is now the most-visited park in the national system, and, like Roan Mountain, it owns the distinction of being shared by the states of North Carolina and Tennessee.

The lessons of prudent land management were not fully learned after the floods at the beginning of the century, however. The days of greatest abuse on Roan Mountain and in the surrounding area were yet to come. After General Wilder's death, his property on the Roan was divided among his heirs, who in turn eventually sold their timber. Most of the visitors to the mountain until then had been scientists and vacationers interested in study, sightseeing, and relaxation, but they were suddenly replaced by logging companies with an eye only toward financial gain. The massive clearcutting they undertook was more than any environment could be expected to absorb.

The Champion Coated Paper Company—later called the Champion Fibre Company and the Champion Paper and Fibre Company—was the principal logging company in the vicinity of the Roan, though it was by no means the only one at work in the southern Appalachians. Champion was begun in Hamilton, Ohio, around the turn of the century by Peter G. Thomson. Thomson's process of making paper and coating it on both sides in a single operation brought him a healthy profit, but not healthy enough; Thomson possessed no forests of his own, so he was hampered by having to buy wood from his competitors. In 1905, he purchased ten thousand acres about seventy miles southwest of Roan Mountain, near the town of Canton, North Carolina, giving him a supply

The ugly aftermath of clearcutting

of spruce for making pulp. Canton had no electricity or central water supply in those days, and it took Thomson three million dollars in borrowed money and more than two years to complete his paper and pulp mill. It took another twenty-one years, until 1929, before his operation reached as far north as the Roan.

Clearcutting provides the most obvious evidence of the kind of damage brought upon the land by logging operations, but even the process of transporting cut logs to the mill can greatly damage forests and streams. Michael Frome described the evolution of methods of moving logs in *Strangers in High Places*:

> The more distant the logger ran his operations from the main line of transportation, the more costly they grew. The mill itself was a relatively small investment. Getting timber out of remote areas was more expensive—therefore the margin of profit depended upon following the shortest, cheapest way. At first, ox teams were used to drag logs to creeks and streams, and on the skid road to the yarding point or deck. They were replaced by horses, which proved faster and easier to handle; besides, a good woods-wise horse often went about his skidding job without reins or words of command. Erosion was caused by clearing lanes for skidders, though nobody cared. And the best way to get lumber down was just to roll it whenever possible. From the high, steep slopes logs were "ball-hooted"—merely started downgrade with peavey, or cant hook. A sixteen-foot log, three feet or more in diameter, would gain sufficient momentum to smash even fair-sized trees in its path, and when it passed through a dense young growth it left a track like a miniature tornado.
> Then there were splash dams and flumes. In setting up a splash dam, the bed of a creek was freed of protruding rocks and fallen timbers, and cleared of all sharp bends. Hemlock logs, snaked to the stream by cattle, were used to build the dam. As the

reservoir grew, animals hauled logs to it over the
skid trail. When the rains came, raising the creek
level, the water would be released by means of a
huge trap door creating a force to splash the logs
downstream. . . . The trouble with splash dams was
that no logs heavier than water could be moved by
splashing and driving, which eliminated oak, ash,
and chestnut. The creek shores and bed were torn,
wrecked, and ruined, but in the helter-skelter of the
day this counted not at all.

Lumber chute, 1934

The scant remains of a spruce-fir forest on the Roan in 1928. A portion of the Board Road is visible in the background.

Methods of removing cut timber from the forests were more sophisticated by the time Champion came to Roan Mountain. Some logging operations were making use of specialized locomotives, log loaders, and skidders, which dragged large loads via overhead cables. But the Roan's unusual geography called for a solution of its own. Champion's approach was to construct a road around both sides of the mountain from Carver's Gap, running right at the elevation where the deciduous and evergreen forests met. It was no ordinary road, but rather one constructed entirely of three-inch-thick balsam boards laid across supports that looked much like stilts. Little or no grading was done for "the Board Road," as it came to be called; its only support was the upright poles. The road snaked around the Roan as if it were floating in the air.

Very few people in the area, particularly on the Tennessee side, remember the Board Road. It must have been a unique engineering feat. I first saw it as a detail in a picture, and later someone gave me a rare close-up photo. I also consider myself fortunate to have actually talked with a man with personal knowledge of the Board Road. He told me that lumber was funneled down long timber chutes to pickup points on the Board Road, where drivers loaded up and headed back toward Carver's Gap. At Carver's Gap, the lumber was transferred to larger trucks and driven into North Carolina by way of the old Calfpen Road, then into Roan Valley and ultimately to Champion's mill in Canton. He described some of the dangers involved as follows:

> I remember many a day havin' to drive the big
> trucks to the spot we had to pick up our load. We had
> to drive them trucks in *backwards* on that old rickety
> road so we'd be facing frontways to drive back out.
> You couldn't go over twenty miles per hour backing
> in, and then you'd have to go a long ways back to the
> farthest pickup point. There were plenty of times
> when the road would *collapse* behind a driver as he

was coming out and he'd have to go just as fast as he
could to get out. Yet on this whole job, no one was
ever killed!

The Board Road wound for several miles around both sides of
the mountain, and it must have been a harrowing midair ride for
drivers in their ponderous, log-laden trucks with the road falling
like a row of dominoes just behind them. All traces of the Board
Road have since disappeared from the forest as completely as if it
had never existed at all.

Champion's logging operations on Roan Mountain continued
until 1937. All trees larger than six inches in diameter were
removed. The forests were completely devastated. More than
thirty-five thousand cords were cut.

Even the rhododendron couldn't seem to hide from the hand of
destruction. In the early days of the century, an entire trainload
was shipped from the Roan to botanical gardens in states to the
north, and it was followed between 1927 and 1935 by more than
a dozen truckloads destined for landscapers in other parts of the
country. Some say that the plateau that supported the largest
natural rhododendron field in the United States was all but
denuded. It seemed that the Roan had been "loved to death," that
it had been beaten and abused beyond hope of repair. The subsequent recovery of both the forests and the rhododendron is strong
testimony for the need for land management, and it is also a tribute
to the resilience of nature itself.

One of the few bright lights during Roan Mountain's darkest
years was Dr. D. M. Brown of Tennessee State Teachers College,
now East Tennessee State University. During 1934, 1936, and
1937, while the last of the area's virgin timber was rapidly disap-
pearing, Brown came to the Roan to study and record the sizes and
locations of the tree species present. He stayed just a small step
ahead of the loggers, and the valuable information he collected
would have been completely lost if not for his forethought. Brown

A rare close-up of the Board Road. This was on the Tennessee side.

used a big box camera to record black-and-white images of the mountain at the tail end of its glory years, shortly before the clearcutting was completed. Like many scientists before him, Brown was puzzled by the Roan's balds, so he planted a group of seedlings on Round Bald, carefully fenced them off, and kept track of their progress to see how they would grow. The mystery of the balds remained intact. Brown's trees came to maturity but never did manage to produce viable seeds. They can still be seen standing in a cluster on Round Bald, though they are beginning to

Dr. Brown's sign on Round Bald

The plot of seedlings

die off now. Brown is credited with completing the first thorough vegetational study of Roan Mountain. Some look upon him as the last of the botanist-explorers who fell in love with the area.

Despite their best efforts, people like Dr. D. M. Brown were powerless in stopping the march of the lumber companies. It took governmental intervention in the coming years to restore Roan Mountain, or, perhaps more accurately, to allow Roan Mountain the time and the peace it needed to begin to restore itself.

Dr. Brown's trees in 1980

THE PARK

*O*ne of the first governmental efforts to protect Roan Mountain's resources came in the 1930s, when the Civilian Conservation Corps (CCC), a Depression-era agency that put the unemployed to work in building public-works projects, constructed a fire tower at Roan High Knob. It was a well-intentioned venture, but also a fruitless one. For one thing, the magnificent forests that the tower was supposed to protect from fire were in the process of being consumed by logging interests, so there was little to guard except brush. And furthermore, a typical day in the tower yielded a twenty-four-hour view of thick banks of clouds. The fog was so dense at "Cloudland" that a fire could probably have been spotted from the CCC tower only if the structure itself were ablaze. The tower was used for only a few years, and it was torn down after about ten years. Concrete pilings still mark its former site.

A popular spot among treasure hunters has long been a sizable dump located below the road near the tower site. It contains trash left by the old CCC crew, and for years it has yielded antique bottles and other forgotten artifacts from Depression days. A shelter for hikers on the Appalachian Trail now stands near the foundation of the fire tower on the former site of an old shelter used by CCC workers.

The CCC fire tower on Roan High Knob

A more effective effort at protecting the mountain came in 1941, when the United States Forest Service purchased approximately seven thousand acres along the top and sides of the Roan. It was hoped that putting a significant portion of the mountain in the public domain would reduce the risk of future abuse and allow the Roan to heal its wounds and reforest its slopes.

Development was slow to come to the area during the 1940s and most of the 1950s. People still traveled to Roan Mountain to see the rhododendron in bloom, to picnic in the meadows, and to enjoy the cool mountain air, but they did so in relatively small numbers. That began to change on January 15, 1959, when the Tennessee legislature passed Senate Bill #17, making Roan Mountain State Park a reality. It was a memorable moment for local residents, many of whom had worked long and hard for the creation of a park.

View from the Rhododendron Gardens, with the fire tower visible to the upper right

Knoxville resident Nancy Tanner had this to say about her Sunday visit to Roan Mountain, as reported in the Toe Valley News *in September 1956:*

That weekend . . . hundreds of people came to see the magnificent displays of wild rhododendron, acres and acres blooming in a setting of blue spruce against a background of mountains rolling to the horizon. When I returned to the hot dusty parking area, crowded with cars from many states, I was struck by the rapt expression of a local woman. "Beautiful sight, isn't it," I said.

"Shore is purty," she agreed. "All them beautiful cars. Every year I come up here just to see them."

To the present date, the majority of the parkland has been acquired through the purchase of private tracts. The first 90 acres came courtesy of a $50,000 grant from the state. The bulk of the land was acquired between 1970 and 1974, when twenty-two tracts totaling 1,947 acres were purchased. The park now stands at a little more than 2,000 acres. Between 1959 and 1974, the only facilities in the park were a small primitive campground and a maintenance area located on the site of the present campground. Once the acquisition of land was completed, however, the park changed rapidly. As a result of development in the late 1970s, it now boasts an impressive array of facilities that contributes greatly to the Roan Mountain experience.

The park entrance is about four miles from the village of Roan Mountain on Tennessee Highway 143. The visitor's center is immediately to the left; the attractive, rustic building also houses

View of Carver's Gap from Round Bald today

the park headquarters. It is at the visitor's center that tourists can pick up information, reserve cabins and picnic shelters, and browse a museum loaded with artifacts from the Roan Mountain area. While the building was under construction, an old water wheel from a local lumbermill was donated to the state. It was split

A 1936 view of the area called "the Stomp," a barrier in the heath bald located up the gravel road past the Rhododendron Gardens. It was said the area gave the impression that it was hollow underneath, so that if a person stomped his or her feet on the site, the echo could be heard going deep into the earth.

in half for transport and brought to the new visitor's center, where it became a permanent and distinctive part of the building once it was reassembled, mounted, and connected to an old corn-grinding mill. The visitor's center soon came to be known by its water wheel. In fact, the wheel is such a local landmark that school and tour groups that come to Roan Mountain State Park for field trips often coordinate their plans by saying, "We'll meet you at the water wheel," or words to that effect. During the spring, summer, and fall, the wheel turns slowly as water pumped from the Doe River cascades across it. In winter, it is draped with snow and icicles.

For those interested in the area's mining history, a trail leads from the visitor's center back into a hemlock forest to the site of the Pegleg Mine. Pegleg is an offshoot of the famous Cranberry

The visitor's center at Roan Mountain State Park,
with the water wheel to the left

vein, once considered among the most remarkable deposits of iron ore in the United States. The Cranberry vein stretches for twenty-two miles and crosses the Tennessee–North Carolina line at Hump Mountain, to the north. Neither Cranberry nor Pegleg is mined any longer.

From the visitor's center, it is another three or four miles up Tennessee Highway 143 to the area where the restaurant and the resort cabins are located. The restaurant can accommodate fifty people. The twenty rustic cabins, constructed in the late 1970s, are nestled comfortably in the woods. Each comes equipped with an array of conveniences: a full kitchen, a wood stove, a modern bathroom, a private bedroom downstairs, a loft with two single beds, supplementary electric heat, and linens. The cabins are designed to sleep six.

The recreation area is located past the cabins. It offers a large swimming pool, tennis courts, playgrounds, a shuffleboard area, and volleyball courts. Behind the pool area is the park's amphitheater, the site of many special events and programs.

The right turn past the pool area leads to the campground. Some campsites are reserved for tent campers, while others come equipped with water and electrical hookups. Restrooms with hot showers are easily accessible from anywhere in the campground. Like the cabins, the campsites were constructed with privacy in mind. Mountain laurel surrounds many of the sites, offering campers a surprising degree of seclusion for a public facility.

The mountain forests that surround Tennessee Highway 143 constitute the majority of the parkland. Twenty-five miles of foot trails give access to the more remote sections of the park. The Roan is a popular destination for cross-country skiers. Some skiing is done in the park's open fields, but most of the cross-country action takes place along Roan Mountain's high ridge line, still approximately fourteen miles beyond the boundary of the park on Tennessee Highway 143. The Forest Service road at the summit is closed to vehicles during snow conditions, and it

Park cabin

Cross-country skier on the Roan

becomes an ideal trail for cross-country skiers. After skiing up the Forest Service road, experienced skiers often like to follow the Appalachian Trail down to Carver's Gap.

In its early days, Roan Mountain State Park seemed to be Tennessee's best-kept secret. Word of the beautiful new facilities was slow in reaching the rest of the world. Once people did learn of the park and its programs, however, they came to visit, and once they came to visit, they returned again and again, and they told their friends and neighbors about the experience. Today, the park's activities include interpretive and recreational programs offered throughout the week during the summer months, from Memorial Day to Labor Day. Naturalist-guided hikes, volleyball and softball games, campfire programs, wildlife demonstrations, folklore and dance programs, and tours of the highlands of the Roan are but a few of the regularly scheduled activities. Special events are organized throughout the year. Among the more popular are the Easter Egg Hunt, the Roan Mountain Wildflower Tours and Bird Walks (in its thirty-third year in 1991), the Junior Trout Tournament, the Clogging Exhibition and Garden Show, the Rhododendron Festival (in its forty-fifth year in 1991), the Fireworks Jamboree in celebration of the Fourth of July, the Fall Naturalists Rally, the Fall Festival, and a Halloween party.

Roan Mountain State Park no longer qualifies as a well-kept secret. It has been discovered by people from all parts of the map. The park's cabins are popular among tourists, and the campground is always busy during the summer months. Every year, more and more visitors attend the special events and journey to the highlands of the Roan. There are days when it seems that the mountain has reached its carrying capacity. It is difficult to imagine a crowded mountain, yet that is certainly the case during June, when thousands of people drive or hike to the top of Roan Mountain to see the Catawba rhododendron in bloom. Extensive signs of overuse and abuse may be in evidence during those times, among them trampling, littering, and the destruction of native flora.

Cloggers at the amphitheater

The Roan once had to attract visitors solely on its own merits, but now, with the park, it has a support staff resting at its feet. Park personnel seek to encourage the intelligent use of resources and to enhance the experience of those who have come to see the mountain's main attractions—the rhododendron, the forests, the balds, the Appalachian Trail, the Cloudland site. The hard use the mountain receives during the peak season is regrettable, and every effort is made to keep it at a minimum, but even at its worst it is a far cry from the wholesale abuses of past generations. Roan Mountain today is in as good a condition as it has enjoyed in many years.

It is a pleasure to say that the sense of discovery that prevails on the mountain has remained intact since the days when hay-fever sufferers at the Cloudland Hotel could be seen combing the balds and the forests for exotic plant life, or even since the great botanist-explorers came in search of their place in scientific history. Visitors today still catch the excitement, still feel pangs of curiosity, and still sense an air of exploration. Many a metal detector has been carried through the woods in hopes that it would unearth valuable information about the hotel and its guests. A dump associated with the hotel has proven quite elusive, as has the famous guest register. Some treasure hunters have found success, though, and it is the possibility of opening another door into the Roan's past that keeps people searching. "For some reason I just felt I should pick up this rock," said one gentleman who was moved to explore the hotel site years ago. "There's a million rocks there, it was real weird. And there, stuck between these two rocks, was this gold coin. Guess it's been there a long, long time."

New forest growth quickly covers the works of man, so there is always the chance that something special waits just beneath the heavy plant cover. It is easy to catch the spirit. I've been prone to it myself. On one occasion, some friends of mine caught my interest with a wild and woolly tale about an important artifact from the Cloudland era that they'd discovered on the mountain. I was eager to see it, of course, and they agreed to take me. The only catch was that they wanted to go at night to add a touch of excitement to the trip.

That day had been crisp and clear, but as night approached a thick fog rolled up the mountain and unfolded on its crest. By the time I met my friends on top of the Roan after dark, we could barely see to walk or drive. I began to feel foolish for agreeing to walk blindly into a forest in a pea-soup fog in search of something that had never been spelled out for me, but my friends tried to reassure me by saying that what we were going to see was well worth any minor discomforts we'd have to suffer along the way. It was a rough walk in our rain gear through the trees, rocks, moss, and holes, with nothing to guide us but our flashlights. I felt doubly gullible when no one seemed to know exactly where this "thing"

Hikers following the Appalachian Trail through the Rhododendron Gardens

was supposed to be; they only knew the general direction. We looked high and low as the fog grew thicker, heavier, and wetter. My hair was dripping from the dampness and my feet were beginning to grow heavy. I was becoming convinced that I was the victim of a bad joke.

Then someone yelled, "Over here!" We hurried around the back of a big gray rock and concentrated our flashlights on a spot where a large, square shape seemed to be growing straight out of the ground. I stood staring a moment, but I couldn't hope to identify the object in the fog and the shadows. "It's an old coffin, an old grave from the hotel," one of my friends explained. "It must have worked its way back up out of the ground. I bet they're all over this mountain!" No one knew quite what to make of our discovery, but it was obvious we'd stumbled upon a significant part of the Roan's history, perhaps even a mysterious graveyard. I wanted to look more closely in the light of day, so I took a moment that night to mark the spot where we exited the woods. Then we stumbled back out onto the trail and down toward our cars.

The fog lifted the next day, and I wasted no time in heading back up the mountain. The route we had traveled the previous night was part of the Appalachian Trail; back in the days of Cloudland, it was also the old road by which visitors wound their way up to the hotel. It was still in good shape considering its many years of service, and I found the going much easier in the daytime. Locating my marked spot was relatively simple; the little pile of rocks I'd made stood out to the left of the trail as I crested a small hill. I turned left into the woods and started climbing.

I walked a good distance without spotting anything familiar, and I was on the verge of turning back and retracing my steps when I saw the big gray rock up ahead. Behind it, half-buried and half-exposed, was a large wooden box that did in fact seem to be trying to wedge its way out of the earth. It was about seven or eight feet long and three feet wide, and it was divided by a partition inside. The part above ground had a large wooden lid. It seemed terribly odd for a casket, so I began to consider other possibilities. My best guess was that the structure was an old toolbox from the days when the original road was under construction, a shelter built by the workers so they would have ready access to the equipment they needed for maintenance.

I was unsure whether to be disappointed in the discovery or pleased with my detective skills. If there is a lesson to be learned from this story, it is that things are not always what they appear to be at night, especially high on a mountain in a thick fog, or that friends who seem to be pulling your leg probably are. From another point of view, I prefer to remember that night as an affirmation of the need to keep digging for information. A forgotten toolbox may not be of the same importance as a graveyard, but it is nonetheless a valuable window into the past. It made me want to learn more.

Roan Mountain has that effect upon people. It seems to breed an air of optimism and possibility. I still remember my first visits, when I was trying to come to some decisions about my future, how lying back in a wonderful carpet of bald grass on top of the Roan seemed to make my problems somehow lighter. I thought back then that everyone should have such a place to go to get back in tune with themselves. Since I have become a full-time resident of the area, I feel it much more strongly.

It will take the care and understanding of all who visit Roan Mountain to maintain its integrity and preserve its unique natural features. The Roan is a special mountain, and a fragile one, too. Yet within that fragility is a strength with the power to refresh the spirit and open the way to discovery. With a little help from its friends, Roan Mountain will be able to experience a future every bit as illustrious as its past.

Select Bibliography

Arthur, John Preston. 1914. *Western North Carolina: A history from 1730 to 1913*. Raleigh, N.C.: Edwards and Broughton Printing Company.

————. 1915. *A history of Watauga County, North Carolina*. Richmond, Va.: Everett Waddy Company.

Bakuzis, E. V., and H. L. Hansen. 1965. *Balsam fir*. Minneapolis: University of Minnesota Press.

Barnhart, John Hendley. 1965. *Biographical notes upon botanists*. Boston: G. K. Hall.

Bartram, William. 1791. *Travels through North and South Carolina, Georgia, east and west Florida, the Cherokee country, & c*. Philadelphia: James and Johnson.

Bayley, W. S. 1922. *General features of the magnetite ores of western North Carolina and east Tennessee*. Department of the Interior. Washington, D.C.: U.S. Government Printing Office.

Beetham, Nellie. 1950. Pollen studies on Roan Mountain. Master's thesis, Duke University.

Billings, W. D., and A. F. Mark. 1957. Factors involved in the persistence of montane treeless balds. *Ecology* 38: 140-42.

Blackmun, Ora. 1977. *Western North Carolina: Its mountains and its people to 1880*. Boone, N.C.: Appalachian Consortium Press.

Bowlick, C. A. 1955. A study of the Cranberry ore belt. Master's thesis, Appalachian State Teachers College.

Britton, E. G. May 1886. Botanical notes in the great valley of Virginia and in the southern Alleghenies. *Bulletin of the Torrey Botanical Club* 13, no. 5.

Brown, D. M. 1941. Vegetation of Roan Mountain: A phytosociological and successional study. *Ecological Monographs* 11: 61-97.

————. 1953. Conifer transplants to a grassy bald on Roan Mountain. *Ecology* 34: 614-17.

Campbell, E. T. 1989. *Tweetsie tales.* Vol. 1. Blowing Rock, N.C.: New River Publishing Company.

Carter, Barbara E. 1979. A survey of the tree layer of the spruce fir forest on Roan Mountain: Carter County Tennessee, and Mitchell County, North Carolina. Master's thesis, East Tennessee State University.

Castro, Philip K. 1969. A quantitative study of the subalpine forest of Roan and Bald mountains in the southern Appalachians. Master's thesis, East Tennessee State University.

Chamberlain, Morrow. 1942. *A brief history of the pig iron industry in east Tennessee.* Chattanooga.

Chickering, J. W. 1880. A summer on Roan Mountain. *Botanical Gazette* 5, no. 12.

Coates, Ruth Allison. 1974. *Great American naturalists.* Minneapolis, Minn.: Lerner Publications Company.

Committee for Tennessee Rare Plants. October 1978. The rare vascular plants of Tennessee. *Journal of the Tennessee Academy of Science* 53, no. 4.

Cooper, Horton. 1964. *History of Avery County.* Asheville, N.C.: Biltmore Press.

Davis, John H., Jr. May 1930. Vegetation of the Black Mountains of North Carolina: An ecological study. *Elisha Mitchell Sci. Soc. Jour.* 45, no. 2.

Dellinger, Clyde J. 1975. *Tweetsie and the Clinchfield railroads.* Morganton, N.C.: News Herald Press.

Earnest, E. 1940. *John and William Bartram, botanists and*

explorers, 1699-1823. Philadelphia: University of
Pennsylvania Press.

Edson, Mrs. H. R. 1894. Frost forms on Roan Mountain. *Pop.
Sci. Monthly* 45: 30-39.

Ferrell, Mallory Hope. 1976. *Tweetsie country*. Boulder, Colo.:
Pruett Publishing Company.

Fink, Paul. 1975. *Backpacking was the only way*. Johnson City:
East Tennessee State University Research Advisory Council.

Frome, Michael. 1966. *Strangers in high places*. New York:
Doubleday and Company.

Gates, William H. 1941. *Observations on the possible origin of
the balds of the southern Appalachians*. Baton Rouge:
Louisiana State University Press.

Gray, Asa. 1892. Notes on a botanical excursion into the
mountains of North Carolina. *American Journal of Science
and Arts* 42, no. 1.

Gray, J. L., ed. 1893. *Letters of Asa Gray*. 2 vols. New York:
Houghton Mifflin Company.

Gray, Ralph, W. E. Garrett, and R. F. Sisson. May 1957.
Rhododendron time on Roan Mountain. *National
Geographic* 61, no. 6: 819.

Hardy, A. V., C. B. Carney, and H. V. Marshall, Jr. 1967.
Climate of North Carolina research stations. Agricultural
Expt. Sta., N.C. State University, Bull. 433. Raleigh.

Harshberger, J. W. An ecological study of the mountainous
North Carolina. *Botanical Gazette* 36: 241-58, 368-83.

John Strother's survey diary. May 1, 1966. *The State* 33, no.
23: 10-14.

Johnson, Kristine D., Hoover L. Lambert, and Patrick J. Barry.
May 1980. *Status and post suppression evaluation of balsam
woolly aphid infestations on Roan Mountain*. Toecane
Ranger District, Pisgah National Forest.

Keith, Arthur. 1903. *Geological atlas*. Cranberry folio.
Washington, D.C.: U.S. Division of Geology.

Lanman, Charles. 1849. *Letters from the Alleghany Mountains*.

New York: G. P. Putnam's Sons.

Lee, W. D. 1955. *The soils of North Carolina, their formation, identification, and use.* Agricultural Expt. Sta., N.C. State College, Tech. Bull. 115. Raleigh.

Mark, A. F. 1958. The ecology of the southern Appalachian grass balds. *Ecological Monographs* 28: 293-338.

———. 1959. The flora of the grass balds and fields of the southern Appalachian Mountains. *Southern Appalachian Bot. Club Jour. (Castanea)* 24: 1-21.

Miall, Louis Compton. 1912. *The early naturalists.* London: Macmillan & Co.

Morley, Margaret W. 1913. *The Carolina mountains.* Boston and New York: Houghton Mifflin Company.

Nitze, H. B. C. 1893. *Iron ores of North Carolina.* Raleigh: North Carolina Division of Geology.

Oosting, H. J., and W. D. Billings. 1951. A comparison of virgin spruce fir forest in the northern and southern Appalachian system. *Ecology* 32: 84-103.

Ramseur, G. S. 1959. The vascular flora of high mountain communities of the southern Appalachians.*Elisha Mitchell Sci. Soc. Jour.* 76: 82-112.

Redfield, J. H. 1879. Notes on a botanical excursion into North Carolina. *Bulletin of the Torrey Botanical Club* 6: 331-39.

Scribner, F. Lamson. 1889. The grasses of Roan Mountain. *Botanical Gazette* 14.

Stuckey, J. L. 1965. *North Carolina, its geology and mineral resources.* Raleigh: N.C. State University Print Shop.

U.S. Congress. Senate. *Message from the president of the United States transmitting a report of the secretary of agriculture in relation to the forests, rivers, and mountains of the southern Appalachian region.* 57th Cong., 1st sess., 1902. Document no. 84.

U.S. Department of Agriculture, N.C. Agricultural Expt. Sta., and TVA. 1952. *Soil survey reports for Mitchell County,*

North Carolina. Washington, D.C.: U.S. Government
Printing Office.

U.S. Department of the Interior. 1931. *Final report of the
Southern Appalachian National Park Commission to the
secretary of the interior.* Washington, D.C.: U.S.
Government Printing Office.

U.S. Geological Survey. 1903. Cranberry folio. No. 90.
Washington, D.C.: U.S. Government Printing Office.

———. 1907. Roan Mountain folio. No. 151.
Washington, D.C.: U.S. Government Printing Office.

Warner, Charles Dudley. 1889. *On horseback: A tour in
Virginia, North Carolina, and Tennessee.* Boston and New
York: Houghton Mifflin Company.

Wells, B. W. 1924. *Major plant communities of
North Carolina.* Agricultural Expt. Sta., N.C. State College,
Bull. 25. Raleigh.

———. 1932. *The natural gardens of North
Carolina.* Chapel Hill: University of North Carolina Press.

———. 1936. Origin of the southern Appalachian grass balds.
Science 83: 283.

———. 1937. Southern Appalachian grass balds. *Elisha
Mitchell Sci. Soc. Jour.* 53: 1-26.

Williams, Samuel C. 1936. *General John T. Wilder:
Commander of the Lightning Brigade.* Bloomington: Indiana
University Press.

Zeigler, Wilbur G., and Ben S. Grosscup. 1883. *The heart of
the Alleghanies or western North Carolina.* Raleigh, N.C.:
Alfred Williams and Company.

INDEX

Fire tower. *See* Civilian
 Conservation Corps fire
 tower
Fires. *See* Burning
Fireworks Jamboree, 149
Flooding, 66, 123-27
Flora-Boreali Americana, 54
Flumes, 122, 130
Forrest, Nathan Bedford, 70, 82
Fort, Tomlinson, 82
Fothergill, John, 51
Fraser, John, 54, 56
Fraser fir, 26, 27-28, 54

Gates, William H., 38, 40
Ginseng, 53, 65
Glaciation, 26, 44
Gouge, John, 107
Grass balds, 32-33
Grassy Ridge Bald, 23, 33
Gray, Asa, 54, 58, 60
Gray's lily, 29, 32, 42, 58, 60
Grazing, 42, 44
Great Smoky Mountains
 National Park, 128
Greene, Grafton, 96

Halloween party, 149
Hampton Creek, 5 (photo)
Hay Fever Brigade, the, 96
Heap (miner), 62
Heath balds. *See* Shrub balds
Highlands of the Roan, the, 11, 23,
 64, 113, 149
"Hot Time in the Old Town, A,"
 103-4
How, Julian P., 100-101
Hump Mountain, 23, 33, 64,
 146

Irwin, May, 104

Jane Bald, 21, 33
Johnson City, Tenn., 7, 10, 23, 65,
 126
Junior Trout Tournament, 149

Landslides, 123, 127
Lee, Fitzhugh, 82

Lightning Brigade, 70, 72, 82
Lilium canadense. See Gray's
 lily
Lilium Grayi. See Gray's lily
Lion's Bluff, 99 (photo). *See
 also* Roan High Bluff
Little Rock Creek, 85, 87
Logging, 60, 115-23, 127, 128-38
Lyre Tree, the, 74 (photo)

McKinley (president), 82
Maher, James A., 124, 126
Maher, Rachel Wilder, 126
Mark, A. F., 38
Marlborough, duke of, 75
May Flood, the, 123-27
Michaux, André, 4, 53-54, 56
Michaux's saxifrage, 32
Milk sickness, 23
Mining, 60-66
Mitchell, Elisha, 33, 56, 58
Mitchell, Mount, 56, 107
Moreland, Wright, 65
Mountain ash, 3-4, 32
Mountain music, 111-13, 114
Murrell, Mrs. N. L., 107
Murrell, N. L., 87, 106

Nathan Bedford Forrest Post of the
 United Confederate Veterans,
 82
National parks, 127-28

Oak-chestnut forests, 26, 36
Overmountain Men, 23

Pardo, Juan, 62
Pegleg Mine, 145-46
Perkins, Ben, 64-65
Perkins, Jake, 64-65
Perkins, Joshua, 64-65
Pippin, Josie, 72 (photo)
Pippin, Sherman, 99
Profile Rock, 19 (photo)

Ragsdale, W. E., 106
*Rhododendron catawbiense.
 See* Catawba rhododendron
Rhododendron Festival, 149